Biblical Studies Student Edition
Part Two: New Testament
2nd Edition

by

Michael J. and Mary C. Findley

© Michael J. and Mary C. Findley 2015
Findley Family Video Publications

Biblical Studies Student Edition Part Two: New Testament 2nd Edition

© Michael J and Mary C. Findley 2015

Findley Family Video Publications

No part of this publication may be reproduced in whole or in part, or stored in any retrieval system, or transmitted in any form by any means, electronic, mechanical, photocopying, recording, or otherwise, without written permission of the publisher. Exception is made for short excerpts used in reviews.

"Speaking the truth in love."

Scripture references are as follows: The Bible: The king James Version, public domain. RV (English Revised Version), also public domain. (Please see the Authors' Note within the doctrinal study materials on Evans' language, Style and Content for information concerning this translation.) The New International Version, from the HOLY BIBLE, NEW INTERNATIONAL VERSION registered NIV registered. Copyright 1973, 1978, 1984 by International Bible Society. Used by permission of Zondervan. All rights reserved. The New American Standard Version: Scripture quotations taken from the New American Standard Bible registered, Copyright 1960, 1962, 1963, 1968, 1971, 1972, 1973, 1975, 1977, 1995 by The Lockman Foundation Used by permission.

Image sources include IMSI Hijack collection, pixabay.com, World Photo Cube, Webtreats, and various public domain sites.

Praise for the Biblical Studies series

" ... Grounded, thorough, well-supported and able to be understood."

"... Solid refutations for common arguments against the validity of Scripture ... "

" ... Pleasantly surprised to find a few new concepts and validations that I had not come across before."

Table of Contents

Introduction to This Compilation of Biblical Study Materials

This collection of biblical studies represents years of teaching to various age groups. Many are correlated with videos available free on YouTube at http://www.youtube.com/user/ffvp5657. Links to specific videos appear in the section they are to be used with. Study questions are included with each section. Short, objective study questions follow each title's reading material.

Note to Reader:

Students will need to write answers in a separate file or on a sheet of paper.

History of the Bible Part Two:

The New Testament and Translations

Accuracy of the New Testament
Authorship and Chronology
Plus Canonicity and Translations

Greek New Testaments
Jerome's Latin Vulgate
English Translations
Spanish Translations
Other Versions

History of the Bible Part Two: The New Testament and Inspiration

Authorship, Timeline for Writing, Earliest Manuscripts

Authorship, Timeline for Writing, Earliest Manuscripts

As the Old Testament was not pieced together by redactors long after the recorded events, so the New Testament did not "develop" from a mysterious "missing" document misnamed "Q." The events of the New Testament happened when the authors said they happened. The people who claimed to write them actually wrote them. They were not forgeries written later. With the exceptions of Hebrews, Matthew, John and Mark, the actual authors are named in the letters or book. Though we might not know the exact time and place these books and letters were written, they are not "cleverly devised fables." They were written during the lifetime of the author and the details written in the various books are accurate. These details help us determine the time and place they were written.

Jesus of Nazareth was born to a virgin. The records of Matthew and Luke are accurate. Jesus was crucified on the Passover between 28 and 33 AD (*Anno Domini*, the Year of Our Lord). If Jesus was born in 4 BC (Before Christ) and crucified in 33AD, He was 37 years old when crucified. If the Gregorian calendar is correct and He was born in 1 AD and crucified in 28 AD, He was crucified when He had just turned 28 years old. The Herods and

Pontius Pilate are mentioned in Roman records. Thousands of places, events, people and objects mentioned in the New Testament are verified and help us place the New Testament in order.

While the exact dates are impossible to determine and good men differ, the gospel according to Matthew was probably the first written of the New Testament books. Written around 35 AD, many believe that an Aramaic version was in widespread circulation, since Jesus spoke Aramaic. The two books of Luke (his gospel and Acts) were penned next, followed by the majority of the epistles. These were written over three decades. The Gospel of Mark followed about the same time Peter wrote his epistles. The Apostle John wrote the last books of the New Testament around 90 AD. We do not know what order, but Church tradition says that John's epistles were written after Revelation and the Gospel of John.

Canonicity and Early Complete Greek Texts

Canonicity and Early Complete Greek Texts

Before all the books of the New Testament were even written, the Roman government ruled that Christians were atheists. Christian writings were burned, Christians were persecuted and their property confiscated. Though some emperors severely persecuted Christians, others did not. The last persecuting emperor, Diocletian, was also the most severe. He executed anyone found with a copy of the New Testament. It is a miracle that anything still exists from the time of Diocletian or earlier. There are many Roman records of these book burnings. During the later Middle Ages, the Church of Rome also burned copies of the New Testament if they were not in Latin.

Rylands Papyrus Fragment

One of the earliest surviving pieces of New Testament Scripture, is a fragment of a papyrus codex containing John 18:31-33 and 37-38, called the *Rylands Papyrus* (P52). This papyrus was found in Egypt, and has been dated at about 125 A.D. It currently resides at the John Rylands Library in Manchester, England. The Chester Beatty Papyri are various papyri collected over a lifetime by Chester Beatty. Though they include medical texts and other non-Biblical texts, the six fragments of the Septuagint and the three fragments of the New Testament are the most important. The total recovered by Chester Beatty of the New Testament were about 300 leaves in three separate papyri. Dated from 200 to 250 AD, these various fragments make up roughly twenty percent of the New Testament. Other tiny fragments of the New Testament from about 200 AD to 325 AD also exist.

When Emperor Constantine reversed Diocletian and stopped destroying the Word of God, entire copies could be preserved. Sadly, many heresies have arisen, falsely claiming that the first ecumenical council called by Constantine and chaired by Eusebius "invented" or "created" the New Testament. All this council did was formally recognize what the persecuted Christian Church understood from the days of John. The twenty-seven books the first ecumenical council "recognized" as the New Testament are the same books we have in our New

Testaments today. The process of canonization was not, as *Wikipedia* and other liberals proclaim "complex and lengthy." *Wikipedia* adds to this error by continuing "Contrary to popular misconception, the New Testament canon was not summarily decided in large church council meetings, but rather developed over many centuries." It is true that the first ecumenical council did not decide what was the New Testament canon, but neither did the canon develop over centuries. Though the canonicity of several apocryphal books such as the *Shepherd of Hermas* or the *Epistle of Barnabas,* and several canonical books such as James were questioned for centuries this is not because the Church was "developing" the canon. These questions arose because of Satanic deception and the inability of the Church to examine the Scriptures due to persecution.

From the time of Constantine to the present there was, however, an explosion of Greek texts and translations. Early Christian sermons and commentaries were also copied. Piecing together fragments of Scriptures quoted in these sermons and commentaries with actual Scripture manuscripts, we have almost the entire New Testament. Though we only have copies, the original sermons date back to the late first century.

Codex Sinaticus

The legalization of Christianity also allowed scribes to copy down complete New Testaments without fear that they would be destroyed. The earliest complete manuscripts in existence are *Vaticanus* and *Sianaticus*. These are complete MSS, not just pieces or fragments. The Eastern Roman Empire, also known as the Byzantine Empire, spoke Greek and used Greek New Testaments until Constantinople fell to the Ottoman Turks in 1626? These Greek New Testaments are called the Byzantine family. These were standardized when Erasmus published The *Novum Instrumentum Omne* ("All of the New Teaching"), the first published New Testament in Greek (1516). It later became known as the *Textus Receptus*. In 1626 the Archbishop of Constantinople, Cyril Lucar, gave the oldest complete New Testament manuscript in the church's possession to the Church of England to keep it from being destroyed by the Turks. Today we call this copy *Alexandranus*. It was used by some of the original King James translators to make a 1629 revision to the KJV. When the Cambridge (1760) and Oxford (1769) editions were published, many of the 1629 revisions were edited out because the editors attempted to go back to the 1613 original.

Jerome's Latin Vulgate

Jerome's Latin Vulgate

In 382, Pope Damascus commissioned Jerome to translate the Bible into Latin, which had become the language of European scholarship. For the *Versio Vulgata* (common translation) Jerome worked from Hebrew and from the Septuagint for the Old Testament. His work took twenty years. He did not complete the New Testament. That work was done later by others and incorporated into his work. It became the standard translation for the Western church after Jerome's death but was not popular during his lifetime.

Augustine protested the Hebrew basis for the translation. He said it would divide the Eastern and Western churches because the Septuagint was preferred in the East. He pointed to an incident where a bishop in Tripoli preached on Jonah from the Vulgate and people rioted in the streets. The Vulgate was the first book printed in moveable type on Gutenberg's Printing Press. The translation into Latin may have been commissioned or later used with the idea of preventing people from reading and understanding the Bible for themselves, forcing them to go to a priest for interpretation. It has flaws, and it is not inspired. However, the Latin Vulgate may be the translation through which more people have come to Christ than any other.

John Wycliffe

Wycliffe's translation of the Scriptures from the Latin Vulgate occurred between 1382 and 1395. Wycliffe was an early reformer. Little is known about the translation work because the Council of Constance (1414 to 1418) ordered the destruction of all records concerning the work and tried to destroy all copies, burning heretics with fragments of Scriptures around their necks and digging up the bones of Wycliffe to burn them.

Wycliffe

It is unknown how many people may have been involved in the work, though Wycliffe and Nicholas of Hereford were certainly involved. It was orthodox according to Roman Catholic belief, but produced without the church's sanction or control, and therefore declared heretical. Thomas More, Lord Chancellor of England under Henry VIII (1478-1535), who was beheaded for opposing Henry's installation of himself as head of the Church of England, used portions of Wycliffe's Bible because it could not be distinguished from “approved” translations.

Martin Luther

Martin Luther published his German translation of the New Testament in 1522. In 1534 he and his helpers finished the Old Testament and the entire Bible was published. He revised the translation throughout his life. When he was criticized for inserting the word “alone” after “faith” in Romans 3:28, he replied in part: “[T]he text itself and the meaning of St. Paul urgently require and demand it.”

Luther

Luther used Saxon chancellery German to make the translation understandable to northern and southern Germans. He wanted the Bible accessible to ordinary Germans, “for we are removing impediments and difficulties so that other people may read it without hindrance.”

Luther's version quickly became a popular and influential Bible translation, especially since it was produced at a time of great demand for German translations. Like Wycliffe's English in his own country, it contributed to the development of the German language and literature. Luther included notes and anti-papal woodcuts by Lucas. The Luther Bible influenced William Tyndale's translation, a precursor of the King James Bible.

William Tyndale

William Tyndale was the first to translate the Bible into English from the original Greek and Hebrew. In 1523 Tyndale asked Bishop Cuthbert Tunstall for help to translate the Bible into English. Tunstall had worked with Erasmus on a Greek New Testament. Tunstall disapproved of an English translation in accordance with the official position of the Church at this time. Tyndale worked and lectured with the help of merchant Humpfrey Monmouth.

Tyndale is believed to have gone to Wittenberg about 1524 and to have completed his New Testament translation in 1525 with the help of friar William Roy. Peter Quentell in Cologne attempted to publish it but was delayed by anti-Lutheran sentiment. Peter Schoeffer produced a full edition in 1526 in Worms. Tunstall condemned the book, threatened booksellers and burned copies when it was smuggled into England and Scotland. Cardinal Wolsey condemned Tyndale as a heretic according to court records from 1529. Tyndale worked on revisions, between Worms, Hamburg, and his finally settling in Antwerp.

Statue of Tyndale

His condemnation of Henry VIII's proposed divorce and remarriage enraged the king. Tyndale was seized in Antwerp in 1535 and condemned to death on a charge of heresy in 1536. Thomas Cromwell's intercession failed to save him. Foxe's Book of Martyrs gives details of his execution. Tyndale "was strangled to death while tied at the stake, and then his dead body was burned" Tyndale's final words, spoken "at the stake with a fervent zeal, and a loud voice", were reported as "Lord! Open the King of England's eyes." Within four years Henry VIII sanctioned the publication of four English translations of the Bible. All, including Henry's official Great Bible, were based on Tyndale's work.

Miles Coverdale

Myles (or Miles) Coverdale in 1535 published the first complete English Bible in print, known as the Coverdale

Bible. He relied on Latin, English and German translations since he did not know Greek or Hebrew. He referenced Tyndale's November 1534 Antwerp edition New Testament plus his Pentateuch and Jonah in English. Jacobus van Meteren helped pay for the Antwerp publication. The Matthew Bible of 1537 included his translations. He oversaw the Paris printing of the "Great Bible" in 1538. London and Paris produced in the same year his Latin New Testament and Coverdale's English. The 1538 Bible compared the Latin Vulgate with his own English translation. He also edited the 1540 Great Bible. Henry VIII placed a Coverdale Bible in every English Church. Though it was chained to the bookstand to prevent theft, every citizen could have access to a Bible.

Coverdale

The Geneva Bible

The Geneva Bible came 51 years before the King James translation. It was used by the 16th century Protestant movement, William Shakespeare, Oliver Cromwell, John Milton, John Knox, John Donne, and John Bunyan (Pilgrim's Progress). It went to America on the Mayflower. Many English Dissenters relied on it. It was the first mechanically printed, mass-produced Bible offered directly to the general public accompanied by an "apparatus" of scriptural study guides and aids. This included verse cross-references, introductions summarizing each book of the Bible, maps, tables, woodcut illustrations and indexes. The Geneva Bible was history's very first study Bible.

The persecutions under Queen Mary I of England (1553 – 1558) drove Protestant scholars out of England to Geneva in Switzerland. John Calvin had created a spiritual and theological republic. William Whittingham was in charge of the translation of the Geneva Bible. Myles Coverdale, Christopher Goodman, Anthony Gilby, Thomas Sampson, and William Cole all participated in the work. The New Testament was complete and published in 1557. Gilby oversaw the Old Testament.

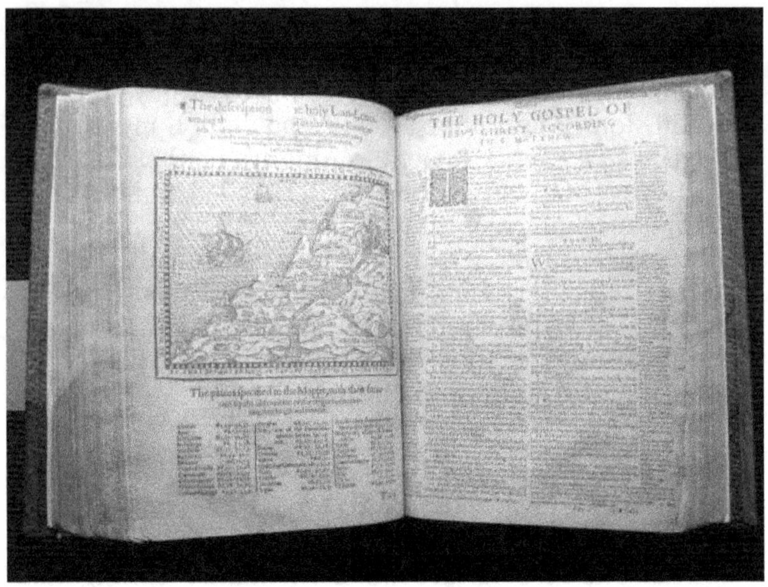

Geneva Bible

The first full edition with a revision of the New Testament, appeared in 1560. The New Testament was not printed in England until 1575. The complete Bible came out in 1576. It went through over 150 editions, the last probably in 1644. The very first Bible printed in Scotland was a Geneva Bible, in 1579. In fact, the involvement of Knox and Calvin in the creation of the Geneva Bible made it especially appealing in Scotland, where a law was passed in 1579 requiring every household of sufficient means to buy a copy.

Some editions from 1576 included Tomson's revisions of the New Testament. Some editions from 1599 onwards used a new "Junius" version of the Book of Revelation, in which the notes were translated from a new Latin commentary by Junius on Revelation.

The Calvinist and Puritan annotations angered pro-government Protestants of the Church of England, as well as King James I, who commissioned the "Authorized Version", or King James Bible, in order to replace it. The

Bishops' Bible under Elizabeth I sought to replace it, as did the *Rheims-Douai* edition by the Catholic community. The Geneva Bible remained popular among Puritans and in widespread use until after the English Civil War. Geneva notes were included in a few editions of the King James version as late as 1715.

Like most English translations of the time, the Geneva Bible was translated from scholarly editions of the Greek New Testament and the Hebrew Scriptures. More than 80 percent of the language in the Geneva Bible is from Tyndale. However, the Geneva Bible was the first English version in which all of the Old Testament was translated directly from the Hebrew.

The Geneva Bible was the first English Bible to use verse numbers based on the work of Stephanus (Robert Estienne of Paris).

The 1560 Geneva Bible was printed in Roman type —the style of type regularly used today, although many versions were produced in the more common Blackletter type. In the late sixteenth century it is likely that the Geneva New Testament cost less than a week's wages even for the lowest-paid labourers.

The 1560 Geneva Bible contained a number of study aids, including woodcut illustrations, maps and explanatory 'tables', i.e. indexes of names and topics, in addition to the famous marginal notes.

Douay-Rheims Bible

Douai, France was a haven for exiled English Catholics. An English College was founded there, and in 1582 a New Testament translated from the Latin Vulgate was produced. The college moved temporarily to Rheims and both towns gave their names to the translation once the Old Testament was incorporated. Gregory Martin, former fellow of St. John's College, Oxford, was the principle translator. William Allen, Richard Bristow and Thomas Worthington proofed and provided notes and annotations. Limited funds prevented the publication of the Old Testament until 1609 and 1610. It had some influence on the King James translators but none in Anglican England after that.

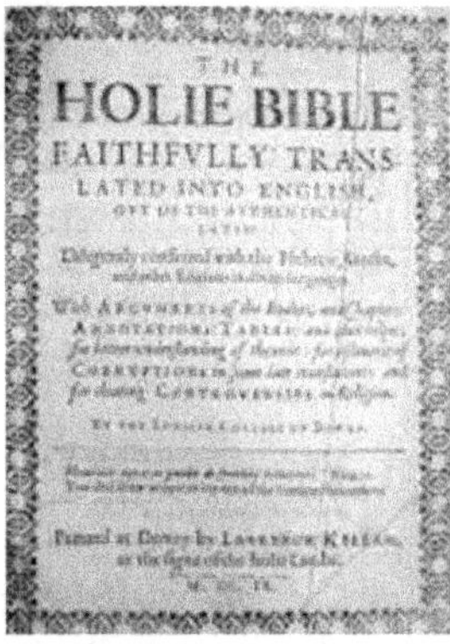
THE
HOLIE BIBLE
FAITHFVLLY TRANS
LATED INTO ENGLISH,

Douay-Rheims 1609 Title Page

"The Holy Bible, faithfully translated into English out of the authentic Latin. Diligently conferred with the Hebrew, Greek and other Editions." Completion of the work required revisions to the Vulgate. Though the English text most used by the translators seems to have been a Tyndale revision in an English and Latin version New Testament, published by Miles Coverdale in Paris in 1538, they had a very different philosophy of translation.

These translators considered Protestant versions to be inaccurate because they claimed to make clear the meanings of texts the Catholic translators believed were unclear. The Catholic translators claimed they used heavily latinized vocabulary to emphasize that these passages were not so easily understood. The effect was a translation few people could hope to understand.

In 1589 William Fulke printed the Rheims New Testament in parallel columns with the Protestant Bishops' version of 1572 with the stated purpose of exposing its errors. The Rheims annotations and his own refutations of them were included. This was probably the most popular version of the Douay-Rheims translation produced and was reprinted up until 1633.

Between 1749 and 1752 Richard Challoner, English bishop of the see of Debra, revised the translation. As a former Protestant he relied on the King James Version. Challoner improved readability and removed ambiguities of meaning that the original Rheims–Douay translators had intended to remain.

The Great Bible

The Great Bible was the first authorized edition of the Bible in English. King Henry VIII intended it to be read aloud in services of the Church of England. It was prepared by Myles Coverdale, commissioned by Sir Thomas Cromwell, Secretary to Henry VIII and Vicar General. In 1538, Cromwell directed the clergy to provide "one book of the Bible of the largest volume in English, and the same set up in some convenient place within the said church that ye have care of, whereas your parishioners may most commodiously resort to the same and read it."

Title Page of the 1539 Great Bible

Tyndale's books were banned by royal proclamation in 1530. Henry promised an officially authorized English Bible being prepared by "learned and catholic scholars." In 1534, Thomas Cranmer compelled ten diocesan bishops to work together on an English New Testament, but most delivered their draft portions late, inadequately, or not at all. By 1537 Cranmer was saying that the proposed Bishops' Bible would not be completed until the day after Doomsday. The King was becoming impatient with the slow progress.

Therefore, the Great Bible relies on the portions of the Bible Tyndale completed but revises parts that English Bishops and the king objected to. Coverdale translated the remaining books of the Old Testament from the Latin Vulgate and German translations, rather than working from the original Greek and Hebrew texts.

The first edition was a run of 2,500 begun in Paris in 1539. Much of the printing was done at Paris but printed sheets were seized by the French authorities on grounds of heresy. The publication was completed in London in 1539. It went through six revisions between 1540 and 1541.

Although called the Great Bible because of its large size, it is also known as the Cromwell Bible after its commissioner, the Whitchurch's Bible after its first English printer or the Chained Bible, since it was chained in place to prevent theft.

The Authorized or King James Version

In 1604, King James I convened the Hampton Court Conference. English Puritans wanted King James I to agree to a new translation of the Scriptures that would address their concerns about the accuracy of previous versions. James demanded support for the Divine Right of rulers and the Episcopal Church structure. The translation was done by 47 scholars, all members of the Church of England. The New Testament was translated from Greek. The Old Testament was translated from Hebrew text.

King James I

The Apocrypha were translated from the Greek and Latin. The translation was completed in 1611, though almost immediately replaced by the 1613 version as typographical errors were corrected. The original printing of the Authorized Version was published by Robert Barker, the King's Printer, in 1611 as a complete folio Bible. By the 18th century it had become the standard English version, even surpassing the Latin Vulgate's use among biblical scholars. A standard text was produced in 1769 and the KJV or Authorized Version remained the unchallenged favorite English version for 250 years.

Revised Version

The Revised Version (or English Revised Version) is a late 19th-century British revision of the King James Version of 1611. The New Testament was published in 1881, the Old Testament in 1885, and the Apocrypha in

1894. It is the only officially authorized and recognized revision of the KJV. There were over 50 scholars from various denominations on the team. American scholars participated by correspondence. The best known of the translation committee members were Brooke Foss Westcott and Fenton John Anthony Hort.

Wescott & Hort

American religious scholars were invited to work on the RV project. 30 scholars were chosen by Philip Schaff and began work in 1872. The American team's suggestions required two-thirds acceptance by the British. Their agreed-upon suggestions were put into the appendix of the RV.

The American team agreed not to publish their version for 14 years. 300 suggestions went into the appendix. The American Standard Version is the American version, published in 1901 after the agreement between the British and American translation teams had expired.

Revised Standard Version

This is a twentieth-century translation (NT 1946, complete Bible in 1952) which states that it derives from Tyndale's 1525 New Testament. It is an authorized revision of the American Standard Version of 1901. It has had a few modified versions, a Catholic edition, and formed the basis for the 1982 Reader's Digest Bible, which removed 55% of the Old Testament and 25% of the New Testament. Its translation of The Hebrew equivalent of the Greek word for "Virgin" as "Young Woman" came under fire from conservatives as undermining the doctrine of the Virgin Birth of Christ. The New Revised Standard Version published in 1989 began the practice of "translating" to promote a gender-neutral agenda.

New American Standard Version

This translation is based on the 1901 American Standard Version. The stated purpose was fourfold:

1. These publications shall be true to the original Hebrew, Aramaic, and Greek.
2. They shall be grammatically correct.
3. They shall be understandable.
4. They shall give the Lord Jesus Christ His proper place, the place which the Word gives Him; therefore, no work will ever be personalized.

The New Testament translation was published in 1963, the complete Bible in 1971, and a new edition in 1995. It is considered the most accurate English translation of the Bible and follows the word-for-word, literal philosophy of translation.

New International Version

The New International Version resulted from co-operation between the Christian Reformed Church, the National Association of Evangelicals, and a group of international scholars. The New York Bible Society (now Biblica) did the translation, releasing the New Testament in 1973 and the full Bible in 1978. It underwent a minor revision in 1984. Today's New International Version was a revision producing a New Testament in 2002 and the complete Bible was published in 2005.

The manuscript base for the Old Testament was *the Biblia Hebraica Stuttgartensia* Masoretic Hebrew Text. Other ancient texts consulted were the Dead Sea Scrolls, the Samaritan Pentateuch, the *Aquila, Symmachus and Theodotion,* the Latin Vulgate, the Syriac Peshitta, the Aramaic Targum, and for the Psalms the *Juxta Hebraica* of Jerome. The manuscript base of the NIV was the *Koine* Greek language editions of the United Bible Societies and of Nestle-Aland for the New Testament. The deuterocanonical books (Apocrypha) are not included in the translation.

Fifteen main Biblical scholars spent ten years with a team of up to 100 scholars from the USA, Canada, the United Kingdom, Australia, New Zealand, and South Africa to produce the original translation. Anglicans, Assemblies of God, Baptist, Christian Reformed, Lutheran and Presbyterian all participated. Translators claimed to balance word-for-word and thought-for-thought translation philosophies. Recent archaeological and linguistic discoveries were said to bring more clarity to traditionally difficult passages.

Later versions have attempted to incorporate so-called "inclusive" language such as gender-neutral elements which have not been well-received by readers. The latest version disregards what Keith Danby, president and chief executive officer of Biblica, called the "underestimated" readers' loyalty to the 1984 NIV and increases the "inclusive" elements.

Spanish Versions

Medieval Spanish Jews created oral translations of the Scriptures and some of these were written down, but the Roman Catholic Church restricted ownership of written Scriptures to persecute Protestants and those who practiced Judaism secretly.

The *Reina-Valera* Spanish translation of the Bible was attributed to Casiodoro de Reina. It was printed in Basel in 1569. Some believe that monks in San Isidoro assisted in this work while avoiding the Inquisition's persecutions. A revision by Cipriano de Valera was printed in London 1596. It was for the use of the incipient Protestant movement and is widely regarded as the Spanish equivalent of the King James Version.

After the publication of the whole Bible by Reina, there was a version from Cipriano de Valera which became part of the first Reina-Valera print (Amsterdam 1602). Many sources have been cited upon which the complete work may have been based, and many revisions were made, including one in 1960, called the "Monterrey Revision Project," aiming at a revision of the original version of 1602 according to the Textus Receptus.

The *Nueva Versión Internacional* is a Spanish translation begun in 1979 and revised in 1999 by Biblica following the same principles and philosophy as the New International Version English Bible.

Other Translations

Many organizations have sought to make translations into every language spoken by man. Missionaries nearly always seek to make a translation into the language of the people they work among if one does not already exist. Wycliffe Bible Translators has carried on this work, and individual missions groups make this a priority. The online Bible resource Bible Gateway says it has over one hundred Bible versions on its site. Not all translations are good translations. Many are imperfect but useful. Our website has an article “What Is a Pig Translation?” exploring some of the problems of translation work.

Review Questions New Testament and Inspiration

Fill-in-the-Blank

1. Which four books of the New Testament do not have authors named within them?

2. Details in books of the New Testament help determine

3. *Anno Domini* is a Latin phrase meaning

4. Rulers mentioned in Roman historical records include

5. The book of Matthew may have first been written in what language spoken by Jesus Christ?

6. Which New Testament book was most likely written first?

7. Two books, one of them a gospel, were likely written next. What were they, and who wrote them?

8. Who wrote his gospel probably at the same time Peter wrote his epistles?

9. Who was the last author to contribute to the New Testament and about what time was it completed?

10. What did the Roman government call Christians?

Matching

Match the lettered items with the numbered items below them by writing the correct letter in the blank beside the number. (More than one lettered item may fit with the same numbered item.)

A. Epistle of Barnabas

B. Rylands Papyrus

C. Sinaticus

D. Eusebius

E. Alexandranus

F. Shepherd of Hermas

G. Vaticanus

H. Novum Instrumentum Omne

I. Chester Beatty Papyri

J. Book of James

1. One of the earliest complete manuscripts in existence

2. An early church father who confirmed the canon of the New Testament already established by first and second century Christians.

3. An apocryphal book from the early church era.

4. A book some questioned as to whether it should be part of the New Testament.

5. Found in Egypt, dated 125 A.D

6. The name of the *Textus Receptus* when first standardized and printed by Erasmus.

7. Manuscript given to the Church of England to protect it from the Turks at the fall of Constantinople.

8. Manuscript fragments dated from 200 to 250 AD, comprising 20% of the New Testament.

1. Translated the Bible into Latin

A. Augustine B. Jerome C. Pope Damascus D. Gutenberg

2. Wycliffe translated the Scriptures into English from

A. Hebrew B. Greek C. Latin D. Syriac

3. The Council of Constance

A. Burned Wycliffe's bones B. Burned anyone with copies of Wycliffe's translation and the copies C. Burned Thomas More for using Wycliff's translation D. A and B

4. Martin Luther's translation

A. was criticized for Romans 3:28 B. became very unpopular C. Removed hindrances to people reading the Scriptures for themselves D. A and C

5. Tyndale's English translation differed from Wycliffe's in that it

A. came from Greek and Hebrew B. it was partly based on Luther's German C. resulted eventually in his execution D. All of the above

6. Tyndale's translation work

A. formed the basis of four sanctioned English translations B. exposed errors in the Great Bible C. was destroyed with no remaining copies D. attacked Henry VIII's divorce and remarriage

7. Myles Coverdale had a part in all the following English translations except

A. Coverdale Bible B. Sinner' Bible C. Matthew Bible D. Great Bible

8. What made the Geneva Bible different from all other translations was

A. It was printed in the Swiss language B. It was printed only in America C. It had study notes and cross references D. It was supported by the Church of England

9. The Geneva Bible influenced all of the following except

A. Martin Luther B. John Donne C.John Bunyan D. William Shakespeare

10. All of the following people were involved in the translation except

A. William Shakespeare B. Miles Coverdale C. John Knox John Calvin

11. All of the following are characteristics of the Geneva Bible except

A. 80% based on Tyndale B. O.T. completely translated from Hebrew C. Roman Type D. cost a year's wages

12. All of the following are characteristics of the Douai-Rheims Bible except

A. It was a French translation B. It used latinized language C. It was translated from Latin D. the most popular version was in a work exposing its errors

13. The Great Bible relied on the condemned Tyndale translation because

A. The Bishops assigned delayed too long in their parts of the work B. Miles Coverdale had been executed C. Thomas Cranmer told the king otherwise it would not be ready until "the day after doomsday." D. A and C

14. The Great Bible was called the "Chained Bible" because

A. It was chained in place to prevent theft B. It was dedicated to martyrs imprisoned for their faith C. It was locked shut when the church was closed D. Henry VIII kept a copy chained to his throne

15. All of the following are characteristics of the Authorized or King James Version Bible except

A. Puritans requested a new translation B. only Church of England Bishops worked on it C. no printer was specially designated to print it D. It remained the most popular English version for 250 years

16. All of the following are characteristics of the Revised Version Bible except

A. Americans had to wait fourteen years to publish differing revisions B. It is the only authorized revision of the King James C. Scholars from all over the world participated D. Many denominations participated

17. All of the following are characteristics of the Revised Standard Bible except

A. The word for virgin in the O.T. was translated "young woman" B. It formed the basis of the Reader's Digest Bible C. It pursued a gender-neutral agenda D. It replaced the King James Version in popularity

18. All of the following are characteristics of the New American Standard Bible except

A. It was a word-for-word translation B. It was based on the American Standard Version C. It followed a literal translation philosophy. D. It replaced the King James Version in popularity

19. All of the following are characteristics of the New International Bible except

A. Scholars from many parts of the world participated B. Scholars from many denominations participated C. It follows a literal, word-for-word translation philosophy D. It relies on recent archaeological and linguistic findings for traditionally difficult passages

20. The *Reina-Valera* translation is significant for all the following reasons except

A. It is the equivalent of the KJV in Spanish B. It was made in defiance of the Spanish Inquisition C. It is partly based on translation work by Spanish-speaking Jews. D. The Monterrey Revision was declared heretical

Research/Thought/Essay Questions

1. Research the meaning and significance of the "Q" document. Include some research about biblical scholarship, the difference between textual criticism and higher criticism, and the authority of New Testament manuscript sources.

2. Research and write about persecutions specifically related to destroying the Scriptures (as opposed to stories of Christian martyrs, which is a worthwhile study, but the assignment should focus on the attacks on the Word itself).

3. Choose one of the Bible translators named in this study and write about the struggles necessary to produce a Bible in the common people's language. Discuss the objections made to doing so and the reasons for believing it was necessary. Discuss how the finished work was spread and suppressed.

4. Reference the article "What Is a Pig Translation?" from the FFVP website and do additional research on the difficulties of Bible translation in cultures with very different frames of reference.

" ... No longer as a slave, but better
than a slave, as a dear brother.
He is very dear to me but
even dearer to you, both as a man
and as a brother in the Lord."
Philemon v. 16

Study Guide for the Book of Philemon

" ... No longer as a slave, but better than a slave, as a dear brother. He is very dear to me but even dearer to you, both as a man and as a brother in the Lord."

Philemon v. 16

The following commentary is designed as a companion to a video set available free on YouTube. https://www.youtube.com/@ffvp5657

Paul the aged, ("an old man" NIV) writes this brief letter to Philemon "with his own hand." Paul usually had someone else act as a scribe or what we think of as a secretary to actually put pen to parchment and write the letter. In Romans 16:22 Paul's scribe Tertius is allowed to sign the letter; "I, Tertius, who wrote down this letter, greet you in the Lord."

The letter is addressed not only to Philemon, but also to Apphia and Archippus. These are members of Philemon's household; however, the exact relationship is somewhat vague. The Greek, as well as the Hebrew, languages do not have the words husband and wife. Instead, these languages use the possessive. For example, Philemon's woman means Philemon's wife. Unfortunately for us, a possessive tense with a proper name can mean sister, daughter or mother, as long as that man is responsible for that woman. Here the grammatical construction of Apphia literally translated means "the sister of us." This phrase parallels 'Timothy our brother' in verse one. She is probably Philemon's wife, but all that we can be certain of is that she is a close relative that Philemon is responsible for in the same way that Paul was responsible for Timothy.

The male name Archippus is also in the possessive, so he is either Philemon's son or father. The phrase "fellow soldier" seems to indicate that he is equal with Paul and therefore a pastor. The phrase "church that meets in your (thy, singular) house," seems to indicate that Archippus owns the house Philemon lives in, so Archippus seems to be Philemon's father. However, if the 'thy house' refers back to Philemon instead of Archippus, then Archippus is probably Philemon's son. Another indication that Archippus is a pastor is found at the end of Colossians, where Paul commands him to fulfill the work he received from the Lord. These are, however, only indications. The Scriptures do not clearly state that Archippus is a pastor.

Every name Paul lists at the end of this brief letter to Philemon; Epaphras, Mark, Aristarchus, Demas, Luke and even Onesimus, is also mentioned at the end of the letter to the Colossians. In the book of Colossians, Paul writes "Epaphras is one of your number." Philemon was obviously a member of the Colossian church. Since he had a congregation in his house (or Archippus' house), and another congregation met in the house of Nympha, Colosse must have had a large congregation of believers.

All that we know for certain about Philemon is that he was responsible for a household, that he had a house with a guest room, that he was indebted to Paul, probably because Paul was the Lord's instrument to lead Philemon to Christ and that he owned at least one slave.

Paul wrote to Philemon while Luke and Demas were still with him but before Demas forsook him for "this present world." As with the letter to the Colossians, Paul was in prison, though we do not know which time or where.

The traditional view of the letter to Philemon is that Onesimus was Philemon's slave who robbed Philemon and ran away. Onesimus met Paul while Paul was in prison, accepted Christ and Paul sent Onesimus back to Philemon.

If this view is correct, then the letter to the Colossians was probably written after this and Philemon had set Onesimus free. In the letter to the Colossians, Onesimus is traveling with Tychicus. Paul writes to the Colossians that Onesimus "is one of you." The two men are Paul's messengers to the Colossians to tell the Colossians everything that is happening to Paul. Some commentators, however, believe that both letters were delivered at the same time.

Paul opens the letter with his position, not as an apostle, but "a prisoner of Christ Jesus." Paul does not use this opening casually or to debase himself. A prisoner of Rome was the only social caste in the Roman Empire lower than a slave. Paul demonstrated his love for Onesimus by pointing out that he was socially beneath Onesimus. Paul also made it clear that even though

Rome forged the chains, he was not a prisoner of Rome, but was a prisoner of the One who was in control of Rome. From the opening greeting, he was reminding Philemon that we are one in Christ Jesus. When we are weak then we are strong. This is not humanist self-abasement, but the proper acknowledgment of the sovereignty of God.

At this time, Timothy is with Paul. Paul mentions Timothy as a brother, an equal brother in Christ that Paul, even as prisoner, is responsible for. Philemon as "fellow worker" is placed by Paul in the same category as Titus, Mark, Epaphras, Luke and every other one of Paul's traveling companions. Philemon is also called "dearly beloved." Paul is not committing the sin of flattery, that is, lying to Philemon to get on his good side. Philemon is truly a giant of the faith.

Paul uses the same salutation which opens all his letters. "Grace to you and peace from God our Father and the

Lord Jesus Christ." Sometimes Paul adds the word mercy, but not every time. Paul uses the same formula, whether writing to an individual such as Titus or Timothy, or a local congregation such as the Galatians or the Colossians. Grace is God giving us good things we do not deserve. Mercy is withholding judgments that we deserve. Peace is the absence of conflict, not with the world, the flesh or the devil, but with God. Grace, mercy and peace all require atonement for our sin.

Paul regularly prays for Philemon, though this letter does not say how often. Other places tell us that Paul prayed night and day for others. In these prayers, Paul thanks his God for Philemon's works of faith and love. Paul claims God as his God and uses every opportunity to proclaim Him. Paul praises Philemon's faith for being placed in the Lord Jesus Christ. Philemon does not have a "faith in faith," a vague belief in something, though we do not know exactly what, but his faith is in Jesus Christ. True faith in Jesus Christ will have results and Paul says that Philemon's faith in Jesus Christ causes him to love both the Lord Jesus Christ and all the saints. Love is not an emotion, but an earnest desire for what is best for someone else. That does not mean that there is no emotion in love, but rather we do what is best for the one we love whether or not we have, at that time, any feelings for the other person.

The next thing Paul prays for is that Philemon will "fellowship his faith." When we think of "sharing our faith," as the NIV translates this phrase, we think of walking up to someone and talking to them about the Lord Jesus Christ. Of course it means talking, but it means much more. It means giving of himself, his time, his treasures, his aspirations. The KJV translation, 'the communication of thy faith,' is probably the best if we understand what that means. It means doing whatever is necessary to get the message across. It means acts of charity, but not just putting some money in a kettle or an offering plate. It means finding out what is best for someone, what they really need and doing it. It really is the same as agape love.

Paul prays that Philemon will "fellowship his faith" not so other believers will benefit, but that Philemon himself will truly know the deep, intimate knowledge of every good thing which we, that is all believers, have in Christ Jesus.

One of the great paradoxes of Christianity is the truth that the more we give, the more we have. Paul says that when Philemon "fellowships his faith" he will experience the full, deep, intimate knowledge of all the good things we can have in Christ Jesus.

Paul continues by praising Philemon's agape love. Not only Paul, but we, Paul and Timothy and all the saints at Colosse are encouraged and rejoice in Philemon's agape love. Philemon himself, as a very dear brother, is responsible for the greatest possible refreshing of all the saints. This gives Paul very great joy.

After the much-deserved praise and the exhortation to Philemon to do even more, Paul seems to changes topics.

"Therefore" (NIV, NASB) or "Wherefore," (KJV) Paul switches from what most commentators view as the "buttering up of Philemon" in the first seven verses to the meat of Paul's message. However, Paul never uses flattery. Everything Paul has written in the first seven verses is not only true and sincere, but absolutely necessary. Because Paul knows Philemon's character, Paul does not have to order him to do what is right. Simply pointing out what is right is all that Philemon needs. That is Philemon's character.

Paul does not say why he could order Philemon; perhaps it is Paul's position as Apostle, perhaps it was that Paul led Philemon to the Lord. Paul simply mentions that he is in the position that he could order Philemon and that he chooses not to. He appeals to Philemon to do "that which is convenient," "that which is proper," (NASB) and "what you ought to do" (NIV). Paul appeals to Philemon for love's sake because Paul is an old man and a prisoner of Jesus Christ. This is the second time Paul mentions that he is a prisoner, emphasizing and contrasting his position with that of Onesimus.

Again, Paul appeals to (beseeches) Philemon, this time mentioning Onesimus by name. Paul calls Onesimus his dear child, his son. This word begotten (NIV born) is the common word for natural birth. It is used over and over throughout the genealogy of Matthew Chapter One and is used in the genealogical portions of Stephen's sermon in Acts Chapter Seven and the listing of the heroes of the faith in Hebrews Chapter Eleven.

There is no question that Onesimus came to Paul an unbeliever and after meeting Paul, the prisoner of Jesus Christ, became a child of God. Paul says that the unbelieving Onesimus was an unprofitable, useless slave to Philemon. After his new birth, Onesimus became profitable to both Paul and Philemon.

The following few verses are the most detailed treatment of slavery in the New Testament. Paul's treatment of slavery bothers most modern commentators. The following comments in the NIV Commentary included in the Zondervan software package is a typical example:

"In this letter, Paul intercedes in behalf of Philemon's runaway slave, Onesimus. His suggestions for handling the matter are difficult to determine because of his obscure and deferential words. At a minimum he asks that Onesimus be reconciled to the household without harsh punishment. He also strongly hints that the slave would be useful to him in the work of evangelism.

Nowhere does Paul openly state that Philemon should set Onesimus free. Nor is it necessary to assume that Onesimus would be freed if he were to join Paul in his missionary work.

I do not find Paul's wording "obscure and deferential." Paul simply does not condemn slavery. Nowhere in the

Word of God is slavery mentioned as the ultimate sin, or even a sin at all. There are over two hundred different Greek words used throughout the New Testament to name various sins and slavery is never mentioned as a sin.

The universal belief today is that the Paul is telling Philemon to set Onesimus free because slavery is a sin. However, when Paul says that he could order (KJV enjoin) Philemon to do what he ought to do (KJV which is convenient, NASB proper), the obvious meaning is that Paul wanted Philemon to take Onesimus back without any punishment. To me, it seems that this is all Paul means. Onesimus, the "free" (runaway) slave, met Paul the prisoner of the Lord Jesus Christ. There he learned that he, Onesimus, was chained in sin while Paul, whose body was chained, was truly free. When Onesimus gave up the chains of sin, he had to make his sin right by returning to Philemon. As a believer, Onesimus' understanding of his God-given responsibility turned him into a useful slave.

Roman prisoners needed someone to take care of them and Onesimus helped Timothy with this difficult and sometimes dangerous care. Even though Onesimus' new birth made him useful to Paul, the right action for Paul was to send Onesimus back to Philemon. This was even more difficult for Paul since Onesimus had become Paul's very heart.

Philemon had helped Paul before. Onesimus was serving Paul the same way Philemon had in the past and Paul the prisoner needed someone to continue this ministry. Paul clearly states that Onesimus was his very heart because he was taking Philemon's place in ministering to Paul. Paul is clearly asking that Onesimus might continue this ministry, but Paul wants Philemon's permission to continue using Onesimus. Even the great apostle Paul does not force someone to do what is right. Philemon must give willingly, not grudgingly or forced.

If Paul expected Philemon to free Onesimus, he would not have told Philemon that Onesimus' departure was to allow them to be together forever. While believers are brothers in Christ who will be together forever, a freed Roman slave rarely chose to stay with a master he had already run away from. Philemon would have Onesimus back as a useful slave for good.

The view that Paul is asking Philemon to free Onesimus is based on the next phrase in verse sixteen where Paul tells Philemon to receive Onesimus back "no longer as a slave." Paul is clearly telling Philemon to receive Onesimus "as a beloved brother," who is "more than a slave." Rather than commanding Philemon to free Onesimus, Paul is simply being consistent with his teaching to masters throughout the New Testament. A typical example is found in Colossians 4:1 where Paul tells masters to treat their slaves with justice and fairness since human masters have a heavenly master which they will answer to.

Though Christianity is a religion of equality, it is also a religion of submission. Wives should submit to their husbands. Children should obey their parents. Church members should submit to their elders. Citizens should submit to the government. Everyone should submit to God and slaves should obey their masters. To masters, Paul emphasizes justice, fairness and compassion remembering that all believers are slaves to the Lord Jesus Christ. To slaves, Paul emphasizes obedience and honor, remembering that all believers will rule and reign with the Lord Jesus Christ and that we are truly free in Him.

Because Paul knows Philemon's character, Paul commands Philemon to love Onesimus as a dear brother. Paul says that no matter how dear Onesimus was to himself, Onesimus was far dearer to Philemon. Paul says Philemon will love Onesimus both as a brother in the

Lord and a man, a fellow human being, an equal before the Lord.

Paul then appeals to Philemon as a "partner." Even though Paul has emphasized his social status as prisoner, he now emphasizes his position as a Roman citizen and an apostolic leader. For Philemon to welcome Onesimus as he would welcome Paul means that Philemon will treat Onesimus as a "partner," not just a social equal. The word "partner" is a business term, so the opening of the next sentence, "if he has done you any wrong," puts this entire section of Paul's letter into a business relationship.

There is nothing in this letter which states that Onesimus has stolen anything from Philemon other than his justly deserved labor. Paul knows that even if Onesimus took nothing else, he owes Philemon that lost labor. So the offer to pay for whatever Onesimus owes is not idle. Paul, as a man of character, pays his debts. An important legal reason for Paul to write this letter with his own hand was this offer to contract Onesimus' debts. Paul wanted Philemon and the courts to be certain that this willingness to assume Philemon's debts was genuine. A letter written by a scribe might be doubted or challenged in court.

Paul again states that he will personally repay any debt Onesimus owes, then he reminds Philemon what he owes Paul. While "you owe me your very self" implies that Paul led Philemon to the Lord, there might be something else involved. Paul then asks for a benefit from Philemon. Since this is in a business section of the letter, the benefit Paul refers to is financial, or at least material.

Traditionally the Church has interpreted this to mean that Paul is asking Philemon to not only spare Onesimus from punishment, but to also send Onesimus back to Paul. "Refresh my heart in Christ" refers not only to the material good of Onesimus' labor but the blessing of Philemon willingly obeying the Word of God. Paul is so confident of Philemon's character that he believes that Philemon will do even more than Paul asks.

Paul's request for a guest room means that Paul fully expects to be released from prison soon. It also means, in this business letter, that Paul will come to settle accounts face to face. It is also a clear statement that answers to prayers are not just fond wishes.

This letter was written after Mark had returned to Paul and once again become profitable but before Demas forsook him for this present world. Luke was with him at this time, so if this were written during the time covered by the Acts of the Apostles, this would be part of the "we" section.

Paul says in closing, as he usually does in his letters, "the grace of the Lord Jesus be with your spirit."

Review Questions For Philemon

1. Which two people are listed as the authors of the book of Philemon?

2. Where did Philemon live?

3. Who was Apphia?

4. Who was Archippus?

5. How did Paul identify himself in the opening statement?

6. What did Paul do with this letter that is so unusual?

7. How many different congregations met in Colosse that we know of?

8. What are the three common elements to Paul's salutations?

9. What does mercy mean?

10. What does grace mean?

11. What is peace with God?

12. What did Paul constantly do for Philemon?

13. What were the two Christian virtues Paul mentions that he heard that Philemon practiced?

14. To whom does Philemon demonstrate these virtues?

15. Paul tells Philemon to continue "fellowshipping his faith." What does that mean?

16. What does Paul say will be the results of Philemon "fellowshipping his faith?"

17. What is the difference between "sharing our faith" and "fellowshipping our faith" in the way we think of sharing our faith?

18. What did Philemon's agape love give Paul?

19. What was the result of Philemon's agape love?

20. After these compliments, what does Paul say that some interpret as a change of subject?

21. How are the compliments actually a necessary part of the subject Paul intends to speak about next?

22. What two things does Paul use as the basis of his appeal to Philemon?

23. At this point, what does Paul call Onesimus?

24. When did Onesimus become Paul's son?

25. What one word does Paul use to describe what Onesimus used to be like to Philemon?

26. After his new birth, what happened to Onesimus?

27. Did Paul tell Philemon to free Onesimus?

28. Rather, what did Paul do for Onesimus?

29. Does Paul condemn slavery?

30. Does Paul approve of slavery?

31. Is slavery permitted in the Mosaic Law?

32. What did Paul want and expect Philemon to do to Onesimus?

33. What did Paul want to do with Onesimus? Why?

34. Why did Paul send Onesimus back?

35. Paul told Philemon to accept Onesimus back "no longer as a slave." What does the phrase "no longer as a slave" mean?

36. What business term does Paul use to describe his relationship with Philemon?

37. As a runaway slave Onesimus incurred some debt to Philemon. What does Paul tell Philemon to do with that debt?

38. What is the last thing Paul asks of Philemon? What does that mean?

39. Who are the five fellow workers who also send their greetings to Philemon?

40. Later on, what happened to Demas?

Apostle Jude Painting by Van Dyck

Study Guide For the Book of Jude

"For there are certain men crept in unawares, who were before of old ordained to this condemnation, ungodly men, turning the grace of our God into lasciviousness, and denying the only Lord God, and our Lord Jesus Christ." Jude 4

The following commentary is designed as a companion to a video available free on YouTube.
https://www.youtube.com/@ffvp5657

v 1 "Jude, the servant of Jesus Christ and brother of James." The short epistle of Jude opens with his name and his authority for writing, which is that he was the brother of James. There were several men in the early church named James. Most people are of the opinion that Jude's brother is either James the brother of Jesus or James the head of the Church in Jerusalem because he is using James as his authority.

The word servant is not what we think of as someone who comes in to clean your house but rather the word slave. It is not just the word slave in the sense of being forced into drudgery, but it is a bondslave. It is the person who, under the Law in the Old Testament, had the option of leaving his master because his term of servitude had expired yet he decided, as a matter of choice, to remain with his master. Jude is a bondslave, a willing slave to the Lord Jesus Christ.

This letter is addressed "to them that are sanctified by God the Father and preserved in Jesus Christ and called." This letter is not to a specific church in a specific location but to the Church of the Lord Jesus Christ throughout the entire world. It is addressing the same problems as II Peter. Many people feel that it was written after II Peter and that many of these problems are worse than they were when Peter wrote.

v 2 “To them that are sanctified by God the Father and preserved in Jesus Christ.” The word “sanctified” means set apart, made holy. If we are talking about perfection, then there is no one who is eligible to meet this high standard of being sinlessly perfect. Sanctified means cleansed by the blood of the Lord Jesus Christ. We are still sinners, even though we are, here on earth at this present time, saints. Not because of any good in us but because of His mercy by which he has called us. We are sanctified by God the Father and we are preserved by Jesus Christ.

“Mercy unto you, and peace, and love, be multiplied.” We find that the word grace, which is in the opening of all of Paul’s epistles, is missing here. Mercy is withholding bad things we deserve. If we have stolen money and we deserve to be thrown in jail and we do not get thrown in jail, after we are caught, that is mercy. Grace is giving to us good things that we have no reason to deserve. Nothing in us qualifies us for this grace. If a child is given a large inheritance from his parents, that is grace. Mercy is withholding the judgment of hell which we deserve. Grace is giving heaven to us, which we do not deserve. And peace is the standing we have with God the Father because of the blood of the Lord Jesus Christ to wash away our sins.

Jude says “mercy and peace.” He adds “love.” He expects us to understand that we have this grace. But love, as opposed to grace, is the outpouring of God’s love. It is not just the outpouring of his emotions and affections the way we think of the word love, but His giving to us what is absolutely the best. It is very similar to the word grace.

v 3 “Beloved, when I gave all diligence to write unto you of the common salvation, it was needful for me to write unto you, and exhort you that and exhort you that ye should earnestly contend for the faith which was once delivered unto the saints.” This verse is the key to understanding the book of Jude. It is the command. It is the purpose. It is the reason. He wanted to write about our common salvation.

He wanted to give what we might think of today as a theological treatise. He wanted to write something like the book of Romans. He wanted to write as Paul had done or maybe the book of Hebrews. Instead, he had to tell us to contend for the faith. That requires us knowing what the faith is. The faith is common to all believers. But it is not a feeling, not an experience, though there are experiences in our faith. It is a body of doctrine. It is teaching. It is understanding what the Word of God is, who God is and what He expects of us.

v 4 “For there are certain men crept in unawares, who were before of old ordained to this condemnation, ungodly men, turning the grace of our God into lasciviousness, and denying the only Lord God, and our Lord Jesus Christ.” Very simply, this is an epistle to the Church. These people who crept in crept into the Church.

Jude is not talking about creeping into houses, though many churches met in houses and so when you are talking about a house church you are talking about the same thing.

These people creeping in either joined a church thinking they were saved or they knew in advance that they did not believe like the rest of the church believed. They were looking at the people in the church as weak or vulnerable or easy prey or else they just hated the Church so much that they disguised themselves as something other than what they were. They went into the Church with either good or bad motives. Either they were deceived or they were extremely wicked from the very beginning.

They went into the Church with the express purpose of turning the grace of the Lord Jesus Christ into sexual immorality. I John deals with this. That is his major argument against gnosticism. II Peter, both I and II Timothy, and Titus all have this. It is a recurring theme throughout the New Testament. It is dealt with somewhat in the book of Acts. In the book of Revelation it is dealt with in more detail as the culmination of the Church Age.

v 5 "I will therefore put you in remembrance." As verse five opens Jude is reminding his listeners, his hearers, his readers, that he is talking about things they already knew.

He is just giving them lessons from the Old Testament. These lessons from the Old Testament are being used to drive home one central point; that they need to contend for the faith. This contending for the faith is nothing new. It has been going on throughout all of human history. He begins with the children of Israel. When God brought them out of the land of Egypt led by Moses, some who believed enough to leave the land of Egypt with them later proved to be unbelievers. Later, God destroyed those unbelievers even though they were joined to the children of Israel.

v 6 The second illustration of God's judgment on unbelievers who crept unawares into the church is verse six. "And the angels which kept not their first estate, but left their own habitation, he hath reserved in everlasting chains under darkness unto the judgment of the great day."

We have the children of Israel who were unbelievers and now we have angels. These angels are exactly what the passage says. They were angels. They were powerful beings who are spirits, but they are real. We have this idea that angels are not real. We think of them as women, as emotional creatures. But every time the Bible talks about angels they have very few emotions. They are also called watchers. They are called various things. Whatever they are called, their power is enormous. God says that these angels which kept not their first estate are reserved in everlasting chains under darkness unto the judgment of the great day. He is referring to the great white throne judgment. There is no question about that.

The chains are not pieces of metal. They are not steel links put together. It is the same idea as when the Bible talks about a key. That key is not a piece of metal which fits into what we think of as a metal lock. Today we understand keys in various ways. A key might be just a code for a computer. It might be just a plastic card which will open up a motel room door. In the same way we are talking about chains. These chains are real; these angels are locked up, they are bound, they are locked in place, but not with pieces of metal, not with links. They are not material. These chains are very real though.

These angels which kept not their first estate are not described anywhere else in the Bible. They are probably those angels referred to in II Peter 2:4; the angels that sinned. Those angels were cast down to Hell (Tartarus) and are bound in chains awaiting the final judgment. God gave them specific responsibilities and they abandoned those responsibilities because they wanted something else. Though we do not know what this something else is, we know that it is an example of the judgment which awaits unbelievers.

v 7 "Even as Sodom and Gomorrah, and the cities about them in like manner, giving themselves over to fornication, and going after strange flesh, are set forth for an example, suffering the vengeance of eternal fire." Chronologically, the judgment on Sodom and Gomorrah happened before the Children of Israel who came out of Egypt were destroyed.

We cannot be certain when "the angels which kept not their first estate" were locked in chains of darkness. There are, however, two basic theories as when this took place. There are people who believe that these angels were chained at the time of the flood. Others believe that they were chained at the death, burial and resurrection of Jesus Christ when He led captivity captive. These people believe that Jesus went down into Hades at His death and He chained these creatures at this time. It does not matter which of these is true or if this chaining occurred at some other time. What we do know is that lasciviousness is condemned once again. These angels "which turned the grace of our God into lasciviousness" are just one more example. Sodom and Gomorrah were the cities which God destroyed in Genesis Chapter 18 during the time of Abraham when God brought Lot and his wife out of Sodom. God attempted to bring Lot's entire family out of Sodom. We get the term Sodomite from that incident.

This is an historical incident. This is not just some sort of story given by way of an illustration. Jude is building here. This is his third example of people that we have to contend with who creep into the church. These are not people outside of the Church. These are people inside of the Church. "Even as Sodom and Gomorrah and the cities about them in like manner, giving themselves over to fornication, suffering the vengeance of eternal fire."

The fire and brimstone (sulfur) which rained down on the historic cities of Sodom and Gomorrah burned themselves out, but the material fire and brimstone are an example of the eternal fire of judgment for those who do not believe.

v 8 “Likewise also these filthy dreamers defile the flesh, despise dominion, and speak evil of dignities.” The sexual sins of those who were creeping into the Church , mentioned by Jude back in verse four are continuing. They are filthy dreamers and their dreams defile the flesh.

Sexual sins are not just a matter of choice. They bring on the vengeance of eternal fires. These dreamers who are defiling the flesh, despising dominion, and speaking evil of celestial beings, do not understand the situation as it truly is. They keep talking about things such as their freedom, their liberties, their personal choices in matters where God said it is clearly a sin. It is a sin that will bring the judgment of God not only on them but also on the people around them, including the church they are in.

v 9 Jude says "Yet Michael the archangel, when contending with the devil he disputed about the body of Moses, durst not bring against him a railing accusation, but said, The Lord rebuke thee." The first and most obvious point is that the devil was greater in power than Michael. We, as Christians, as believers, as those who are of the faith once for all delivered unto the saints, do not have the power to go up against Satan, celestial beings, the powers of darkness in our own strength. We should not be like these people who despise dominions and speak evil of dignities. They really do not know what they are talking about.

There is no place else in the Scriptures that says that Michael the archangel disputed with the devil over the body of Moses. We do not know anything else other than what Jude tells us right here about this individual action. We do not know what it means to dispute over the body of Moses. We do not know what happened to the body of Moses. There's nothing in the Scriptures and the traditions which have been handed down to us are so fanciful and ridiculous that they should be ignored.

v 10 "But these speak evil of those things which they know not: but what they know naturally, as brute beasts, in those things they corrupt themselves." Very simple, very straightforward. Again, Jude is talking about sex. But he is talking about far more. They speak evil of things which they do not know. What do we know about evil spirits? Very little. What these people do know they learned through their natural instincts. However, they use this knowledge to debase themselves, not to do what they should do. Even Emperor Penguins take care of their young in the bitter cold. Yet human beings who have rejected the Law of God will do anything to please themselves, including killing their own children. As the Apostle Paul said, they have made their appetites their gods.

v11 a "Woe unto them! For they have gone in the way of Cain, and ran greedily after the error of Balaam for reward, and perished in the gainsaying of Core." Three people from very different time periods. Cain goes all the way back to the creation. Adam and Eve's son Cain rose up and slew his brother Abel. The way of Cain is not only murder, but stubborn selfish pride, doing it my way. This attitude is glorified in the song Frank Sinatra popularized, "My Way."

"Greedily after the error of Balaam for reward." The Mesopotamian prophet Balaam was called by Balak, the King of Moab, to curse the Children of Israel when Moses had them at the Jordan River ready to cross into the Promised Land. Balaam came and said, "I cannot do anything except what the Lord commands me." He pronounced God's blessing on Israel because God commanded Israel to be blessed. But he still wanted the reward which Balak offered to him. He came up with a plan to destroy the Children of Israel by having the Children of Israel go after the women of Moab in sexual intercourse as part of the worship of their gods.

Phinehas, the son of Eleazar the high priest, the son of Aaron, took a spear and ran it through one of the children of Israel while he was having sexual intercourse with one of the women of Moab as part of a public worship service. The Scriptures say that a leader from the tribe of Simeon brought a Moabite woman publicly into the camp while the rest of Israel was mourning and repenting of this great sin. Then they went into a tent. Phinehas followed them into the tent where he ran a spear through them to show what an abomination it was in the sight of God. Again, they were corrupting themselves naturally with the way they knew.

v 11b The last part of verse eleven says that they have perished in the gainsaying of Korah. Gainsaying is not a word which we use today. It means to speak against. It means rebellion. Korah got the idea that he was just as good as Moses. Unlike Balaam who knew that he just wanted the money, and unlike Cain, whose pride just hardened his heart so that he said, “I do not care what God wants, I am going to do it my way,” and he rose up in a fit of rage and he killed his brother, Korah was probably self-deceived.

We do not know that. The Scriptures do not say that. But why in the world would Korah, after witnessing all of the plagues of Egypt, the destruction of the Egyptians, the power of God, the crossing of the Red Sea, Mount Sinai, the worship of Baal and the golden calf that Aaron had made, would he then come up to Moses and say that Moses was taking too much on himself and that “God speaks to me as much as God speaks to you.” Is Korah a fool? Or is he simply saying that he has been deceived and that “I believe that what I am saying is right?” He convinced other people to go along with him. There were many men with their families, their wives, their women, their children, complete families who were destroyed in this rebellion. So I see Jude mentioning three different things here: the hardened sinner, Cain, who just wants his own way no matter what, the greed of Balaam, and having that greed corrupt you, whatever position you are in life, and Korah, letting power corrupt you and blinding you to your actual standing before God.

vv 12&13 “These are spots in your feasts of charity, when they feast with you, feeding themselves without fear: clouds they are without water, carried about of winds; trees whose fruit withereth, without fruit, twice dead, plucked up by the roots. Woe to them.” These people are spots in your feasts of charity. These feasts of charity are debated a great deal among believers today. The Apostle Paul dealt with the problems of these feasts of charity in the Corinthian church. When believers met together in the early Christian Church part of the worship service they had a meal which they called a love feast. If it was like a potluck supper where there was plenty of food and everyone is welcome, that is great. That is what Paul was encouraging and had in mind.

But love feasts frequently degenerated, as the situation in Corinth had, into a way of people saying that they were better than others by bringing better food and not sharing it. Jude is not dealing with that issue. The situation Jude is dealing with is a true love feast. These people were gathering together in true Christian love. But it says that these men who had crept into the Church unawares were feasting with them but were only feeding themselves.

Jude describes them as "feeding themselves without fear: clouds they are without water, carried about of winds; trees whose fruit withereth, without fruit, twice dead, plucked up by the roots; raging waves of the sea, foaming out their own shame; wandering stars, to whom is reserved the blackness of darkness for ever." Each one of these points is an illustration of something destructive, something which has no value to other people.

For example, a star is something that can be relied on confidently for navigation. If you place your confidence in a wandering star, then you will get lost. We are to be steady, year in and year out, a beacon for others. Wandering stars destroy that confidence.

v 14 "And Enoch also, the seventh from Adam, prophesied of these, saying, Behold, the Lord cometh with ten thousands of his saints." First, many people say that this is a direct quote from the book of Enoch. A close look reveals some subtle differences between this passage and the apocryphal book of Enoch. The most likely explanation is a common source for both Jude and the book of Enoch. It might even be possible that the book of Enoch was written after the book of Jude and uses Jude as its source.

Under the inspiration of the Holy Spirit, Jude penned down the information that he had. Enoch, the seventh from Adam, is prophesying that the Lord is coming with ten thousands of His saints. Who are his saints? If you have accepted Jesus Christ as your personal Saviour, you are one of his saints. We are, each one of us, one of his saints. There is no question that the saints of all the ages are going to be returning with the Lord.

v 15 When the Lord comes with ten thousands of His saints, He is going "to execute judgment upon all, and convince all that are ungodly among them of all their ungodly deeds which they have ungodly committed, and of all their hard speeches which ungodly sinners have spoken against him."

The word ungodly, which is repeated over and over in the book of Jude and is repeated four times in this verse, verse 15, means very simply that all of their thoughts, their life goals, their ambitions, their desires are opposed to God.

There are two kinds of ungodliness which we recognize today. First there are people who live apart from God but are not openly opposed to Him. They are trying to live one foot in the world and one foot in the church. That is not what these people are. The word ungodly in this sense refers to people who are opposed, shaking their clenched fists, to God. Remember, we are to contend with these people. We are to contend for the faith.

v 16 "These are murmurers, complainers, walking after their own lusts; and their mouth speaketh great swelling words, having men's persons in admiration because of advantage." The Elizabethan English of the King James translation makes this a little difficult to understand. The term murmurers means someone who sits around and complains all the time with their hand over the front of their mouth. Gripers, murmurers and complainers are kind of the same thing.

But walking after their own lusts? What are we talking about? Jude does not just mean sex. He means their appetites. Paul mentions this. Peter mentions this. These are people doing exactly what they want instead of what they ought to do. There is no question that they understand what they are doing and that they do not care what people think of them. They do not care what God thinks of them. They have one thing and one thing only for a goal; self-fulfillment, self-indulgence.

Remember that the Bible does not mince words and that it does not speak in pyschobabble. When it is talking about people and their own desires, these desires are contrary to the word of God. This does not mean that we should never do anything we want. It is not saying that it is a sin to go on vacation, that it is a sin to get married, that it is a sin to do something which we enjoy. That is not what Jude is saying.

Jude is saying that the desire for power, to go our own way, and greed, come between us and God. These sins are filling the church and Jude is commanding those who are not caught up with these sins to contend with these people to keep them from sinning. Jude is giving example after example of those we must contend with.

v 17 "But, beloved, remember ye the words which were spoken before of the apostles of our Lord Jesus Christ."

That says it all right there. Remember the words which the Lord's apostles spoke. We do not have an option as to whether or not we should be doing our own thing. We need to be studying, studying, studying; becoming more like the Lord Jesus Christ.

The studying which is being talked about here, the studying which we find throughout the Word of God, is not sit, soak and sour. It is knowing how to give an answer to every man. We need to know more than just the Bible. We need to know the Bible, but we also need to know geology and history. We need to know about automechanics and carpentry. We need to know how to cook, how to take care of our homes, how to do things properly so that we can live a life that is peaceful. We need to live lives which are decent and in order.

v 18 "How that they told you there should be mockers in the last time, who should walk after their own ungodly lusts." Yes, we have to remember the words of the apostles, and all of the words of the apostles are important, but Jude wants us specifically to remember the last times. And what are the last times? The times we are living in, the times from the death, burial and resurrection of the Lord Jesus Christ until His return in the clouds in the air. These things are described in I Corinthians 15 and I Thessalonians 4, some of the most important passages in the Scriptures.

These men are going to be mocking God, walking after (and here is that word again) their own ungodly lusts. Jude is saying the same message over and over and over again and yet so many people still do not get it. They still do their own thing. This is a message against those people. It is not just saying that they are wrong, but it is a command for those who love the Lord Jesus Christ with all their hearts to contend for the faith. And contending for the faith is looking at these people who are walking after their own ungodly lusts and talking to them, praying with them, doing whatever is necessary to keep them from these sins.

v 19 “These be they who separate themselves, sensual, having not the Spirit.” It is very simple. It is very plain. It is easy to understand. God has given us the command that we are to walk separate, holy lives. But we are separated unto God and unto God’s Word and unto God’s people. When Jude says they separate themselves, he is talking about people who go apart, away from God’s people, wanting nothing to do with God’s people; no fellowship, no desire, no love. They are after their own interests. Many times they have great followings. We have cult after cult after cult throughout all of the history of the Church of people who have come up with their own ideas contrary to the Scriptures, who seduce people and have huge followings. They do not have the Spirit and Jude says right here that they are sensual. They are connected to this earth. They are earthly, minding earthly things.

v 20 “But ye, beloved, building up yourselves on your most holy faith, praying in the Holy Ghost, Keep yourselves in the love of God, looking for the mercy of our Lord Jesus Christ unto eternal life." Pretty simple. Pretty straightforward. We are to build up ourselves. How do we build up ourselves? We do good works. But we only know what good works are by being directed by God's Holy Spirit as we read God's Word. You can make the Word of God say anything; literally. There is nothing which you cannot justify by some little fragment or passage from Scripture. But building up ourselves in the most holy faith is comparing Scripture with Scripture. It is having godly men help us out with their understanding, studying the original languages, studying the actual meaning of the text, putting it in its proper context, knowing the history of the times, knowing the culture and what that means. It is living that life daily, going after others, trying to snatch them from the fire.

v 21 "Keep yourselves in the love of God, looking for the mercy of our Lord Jesus Christ unto eternal life." To keep yourself means to keep yourself from being contaminated with this world. That does not mean, as Paul was so clear, to become hermit or a nun or a monk or to lock yourself up away from the world. No, that is not what Jude means.

Keeping yourself unspotted from the world means as the Lord Jesus Christ kept Himself unspotted from the world. He spent all of His time out in the world, out in the fields, talking with people, going from town to town, preaching the gospel. And yet people today think that keeping themselves means isolating themselves.

We understand what the love of God is. We are looking for the mercy of our Lord Jesus Christ. And eternal life is more than just the sweet by and by. When Jude talks about eternal life, we are looking for our resurrected body and more. It is the quality of life, it is the sweet fellowship with Him, it is the fellowship with other believers in the Lord Jesus Christ.

vv 22-25 "And of some have compassion, making a difference." There is no question that we should have compassion to all. But this "compassion making a difference" is for that person who is in great need, and we are so moved that we go out and intervene and help that person. It might be providing food, but rarely is that the issue. It is usually time, energy, effort, doing things for someone who needs them and cannot do them for themselves.

"And others save with fear, pulling them out of the fire; hating even the garment spotted by the flesh." This is the opposite of verse 22, of some have compassion; others save with fear. You are intervening in verse 23 pulling them out of the fire, hating even the garment spotted by the flesh. You are intervening in situations where they might not want you. You are going into places that are dirty and standing up to what is wrong.

And you are standing up in a way that makes a difference. You are not trying to get yourself killed but you are trying to help somebody. It is no good to try to save a drowning person if both of you end up drowning. Whatever you do, do it in an intelligent manner. If you see someone drowning you throw him a rope. You hold a stick out. You toss him a coat as a rope, so you can pull him in. You do not put yourself in danger. But it does not mean that you just sit back.

It is more than just the compassion of helping him out somehow. They are in a bad situation and you have to change it. And you have to make them understand that they have to change. "Now unto him that is able to keep you from falling, and to present you faultless before the presence of his glory with exceeding joy, To the only wise God our Saviour, be glory and majesty, dominion and power, both now and ever. Amen."

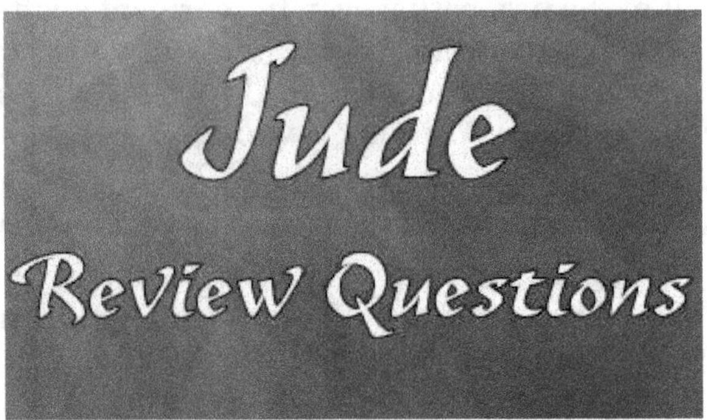

Jude Study Questions and Answers

1. Jude opens this short epistle by mentioning his brother. What is his brother's name?

2. What two reasons would Jude have for mentioning his brother?

3. What does the word translated "servant" really mean?

4. What other New Testament book addresses the same problems as Jude?

5. What does sanctified mean?

6. What does the word mercy mean?

7. What does the word peace mean?

8. When God gives us His love, what is He giving us?

9. What word, which is not found in Jude's opening, has a similar meaning to love?

10. What command does Jude give us which is the key to this epistle?

11. What is “the faith which was once delivered unto the saints?”

12. Who are “the saints?”

13. There are “certain men who crept in unawares.” What did they creep into?

14. What did they want to turn the Grace of the Lord Jesus Christ into?

15. These people who crept in were from the beginning either self-deceived or what?

16. What does Jude want to remind his readers of?

17. Jude begins with three examples from the Old Testament. What are they?

18. In each example Jude mentions a specific sin which caused God to step in and execute immediate judgment. What are the three sins and who do they go with?

19. Jude calls these men filthy dreamers. What is the meaning of this phrase?

20. What two sins does Jude list as coming from filthy dreaming?

21. What do these kinds of people spend all of their time talking about?

22. What is the name of the archangel named by Jude?

23. Who did he contend with?

24. What was the point of contention?

25. What did the archangel say to gain the victory?

26. What is happening to people who speak evil of things they do not understand?

27. What does Jude compare them to?

28. What word does Jude use, which is used frequently in Revelation, as a pronouncement of judgment?

29. Name the three Old Testament sinners Jude uses as examples.

30. How does the KJV describe their sins?

31. What is the best way of translating those sins into our way of thinking?

32. What were the "love feasts" or "feasts of charity" of the early church?

33. What was the problem with the feasts of charity which Paul dealt with in Corinth?

34. What was the problem with the feasts of charity which Jude dealt with?

35. Jude uses four illustrations for these men. What are they?

36. Who does Jude say prophesied of these men?

37. What did he say?

38. What will the Lord do?

39. What are the two general types of ungodly people?

40. The KJV calls these men murmurers. What other two words mean almost the same thing?

41. "Walking after their own lusts" means much more than sexual immorality. What is the expanded meaning of that phrase?

42. Is marriage a sin?

43. What does Jude command us to do with these men?

44. What is the purpose of our contending with these men?

45. What is the specific sin Jude mentions in v 16 according to the KJV?

46. What does that mean?

47. What words does Jude command us to remember?

48. What are we supposed to study to become more like?

49. What were we told would come in the last time?

50. When are the last times?

51. Once again, what does Jude say that these mockers are walking after?

52. What one word does Jude use to describe those who separate themselves and do not have the Spirit?

53. What does that word mean?

54. Next, what does Jude command us to do?

55. What is our authority for understanding how to do these things?

56. What does Jude mean when he says that we are to keep ourselves in the love of God?

57. What is eternal life?

58. The two final words Jude uses for ministering to others are compassion and fear. They are the opposite types of ministry. What do they mean?

Revelation

Study Guide For the Book of Revelation

"If those days had not been cut short, no one would survive."

Matthew 24:22.

Sources used for research in preparing this book are: John Seiss' Commentary on Revelation, Babylon by R. H. Mount and The Bible Knowledge Commentary, edited by Walvoord and Zuck, a commentary on the entire Bible. I consulted Lenski's Commentary on Revelation for familiarity with the amillennial position. For koine Greek lexicons I used Bauer's Greek-English Lexicon, translated by Arndt and Gingrich, and Joseph Thayer's Greek-English Lexicon. I also consulted Zondervan's Reference Software and the Logos Library System and the dissertation of Dr. Charles Smith.

Introduction to Revelation

The original 67 video lessons averaged around 3-6 minutes each and were made over several years. The 34 YouTube videos are roughly 10 minutes each and combine these original segments, though the divisions can still be clearly seen and followed.

https://www.youtube.com/@ffvp5657

(Our apologies, but segment 28 was damaged and we cannot find a backup to replace it. Hopefully we will restore it at a later time.)

By the grace of God, this is our attempt to make the teaching of the book of Revelation more interesting. Please read the passage in the Word of God first before watching the video commentary for that section. The first two lessons, however, are an overview of the entire book of Revelation so these two introductory lessons do not have a short passage to go along with them.

We believe the Bible means what it says and says what it means. These lessons are strongly opposed to the popular heresies which "spiritualize" this book of the Bible. Today, most people call the literal view of Revelation Premillennialism. The early Church believed this unanimously and called it Chiliasm. Obviously there are symbols throughout this book. First, we believe that the symbols used and developed throughout the Bible are used in the same way in the book of Revelation. For instance, the sword of the Spirit is the Word of God. The sword pictured in Revelation as coming out of the mouth of the Lord Jesus Christ is obviously the Word of God. Secondly, we believe that some symbols introduced in the book of Revelation are described as symbols and explained in the same passage where they are introduced. For example, the woman in Chapter Twelve is called a sign and gives us enough detail to properly interpret the sign. Anything else that is not clearly identified as a sign, either in the book of Revelation or elsewhere in the Word of God, is to be taken to be what it says.

Author's note: The book of Revelation is widely known as "the happy hunting ground of theological crackpots." For this reason, I have not taught this book of the Bible in over 20 years of teaching. I was asked to teach it and this is an attempt to honor that request.

Part One: General Introduction, Overview and Definitions

Part One: General Introduction, Overview, and Definitions

These notes use one of 3 English translations:

1) The Authorized or King James Version. Though never authorized by King James, he did permit a new translation, as long as the translators paid for it out of their own pockets. The original translation was completed in 1611. The 1st revision was published in 1613, though the changes were minor. The most important revision was the 1629 incorporation of the recently acquired (1626) Alexandrinus copy of the NT. So many revisions followed that there was no standard until Queen Victoria authorized a revision committee in the 1830's. Authorization in England is similar to what Americans think of as a copyright. One result of Queen Victoria's revision committee was a standard version of the older translation with modernized spelling. Queen Victoria authorized this version, which followed the 1629 revision. This is the popular King James Version that we have today. It is the greatest work of literature in the English Language. It was developed for public reading and has a beauty that no modern translation even attempts to copy.

2) The New American Standard Translation. Translated by the Lockman Foundation and covered by a series of copyrights starting in 1960, this is the most literal translation into English ever made. With little or no

priority for literary value, this translation does not 'read' well. Since computers and modern study helps allow direct access to Greek and Hebrew without knowing either language, the NASB is not very popular, even among scholars and Pastors.

3) The New International Version. Translated by the International Bible Society and covered by a series of copyrights starting in 1973, this is the most popular version in English today. No statistics are available for sales of the KJV; excluding the KJV, more copies of the NIV are sold than all other English translations combined. Estimates are that the NIV is more widely read than any other English translation, including the KJV. The NIV is a 'thought' translation, attempting to translate the kernel idea into a very readable modern English rather than attempting an 'equal word' translation as the Lockman foundation did with the NASB. While not possessing the timeless literary beauty of the KJV or the exacting standards for accuracy of the NASB, the NIV is the most conservative, readable modern English translation as of the 1985 revision, which is the version referenced in this work. After that time, the revisions have become more and more concerned with political correctness and gender neutrality than accuracy. Unless otherwise noted, Scripture quotations in these notes are from the 1985 revision NIV.

Literal Interpretation

Revelation means what it says and says what it means. As the culmination of God's written Word, it relies on symbols established throughout the Word of God. See the attached appendix for basic meanings of common symbols.

I firmly believe that any symbol introduced in the book of revelation is explained where it is introduced. The basic principle of interpretation for the entire Scriptures hold true for Revelation. Deut. 29:29, "The secret things belong to the LORD our God, but the things revealed belong to us and to our children forever, that we may follow all the words of this law."

One guiding principle of the Book of Revelation is that it is written as we write history books. The same time period (time, times and half a time (12:14 from Daniel 4:16,23,25,32 7:25 9:25 12:7); 42 months (11:2 & 13:5); 1260 days (11:3 & 12:6)) is referred to repeatedly, only from different points of view. Most historians use this technique. For example, A History of Westward Expansion has many chapters on the weapons, naval, air, political, home fronts, European theater, pacific theater, propaganda, and medical.

Timeline—Overview

Timeline -- Overview

Daniel 9:24—"Seventy 'sevens' (can also be translated weeks: each week or seven is a period of seven years) are decreed for your people and your holy city..."

Daniel 9:25—"Know and understand this: From the issuing of the decree to restore and rebuild Jerusalem (This is not the general decree for all people to return to their homelands issued by Cyrus in 535 BC [Ezra 1], nor is it the decree of Darius [Ezra 6] to rebuild the temple. This is the much later request of Nehemiah granted by Artaxerxes in Nehemiah 2) until the Anointed One, the ruler comes, (Jesus Christ) there will be seven 'sevens,' and sixty-two 'sevens.'

(483 years according to the Jewish calendar) After the sixty-two 'sevens,' the Anointed One will be cut off and will have nothing. (The death, burial and resurrection of Jesus Christ, according to the Scriptures.) The people of

the ruler who will come will destroy the city and the sanctuary.

(Double prophecy: First, the Roman armies under Titus destroyed Jerusalem in A.D. 70. Second, the armies of the Beast of Revelation will again destroy Jerusalem and the temple, which means that the temple will be rebuilt.)

The resurrection of Christ began the Church Age, the outpouring of God's Holy Spirit (Acts 2:17, 33). For unbelievers He convinces of sin and woos them to salvation. For believers, He empowers them to godliness. The Church Age is the gap in Daniel, which will end with the Rapture. I Corinthians 15:51— Listen, I tell you a mystery: We will not all sleep, but we will all be changed - in a flash, in the twinkling of an eye, at the last trumpet. For the trumpet will sound, the dead will be raised imperishable, and we will be changed.

I Thessalonians 4:16,17— For the Lord himself will come down from heaven with a loud command, with the voice of the archangel and with the trumpet call of God, and the dead in Christ will rise first. After that, we who are still alive and are left will be caught up together with them in the clouds to meet the Lord in the air. And so we will be with the Lord forever.

The Church will then appear before the bema, which is translated "judgment seat" in Romans 14:10 and II Corinthians 5:10. It is the word for the place where Pilate sat in judgment of Christ Jesus. It is usually translated "court." Outside of the New Testament, this word is used of the seat of the judge of athletic contests. This is the time we will receive our rewards for faithful obedience to Jesus Christ.

After the Church is raptured, the people on whom the Spirit has been poured will no longer be on earth. Those left behind will be sent "a powerful delusion so that they will believe the lie." (II Thessalonians 2:11) At this time the lawless one, the man of sin, the Antichrist (and his governmental organization, the beast) will be revealed.

The beginning of what is known as the Tribulation is what follows in God's timetable. Daniel 9:27—"He (the beast) will confirm a covenant with many for one 'seven.'" What is this covenant or treaty? It is the re-establishing of sacrifices in the rebuilt temple. "In the middle of the 'seven' he will put an end to sacrifice and offering."

Daniel 11:31— "His armed forces will rise up to desecrate the temple fortress and will abolish the daily sacrifice. Then they will set up the abomination that causes desolation."

From our point of view, the next event on God's timetable is the Rapture of the Church. The revealing of the lawless one will follow that. He will make a seven-year treaty with many to rebuild the temple and restart the daily temple sacrifices. This treaty begins what is known as the Tribulation. The Tribulation begins as a time of great peace (The first rider on a white horse with a crown and a bow, but no arrows; second rider takes peace from the earth). Midway into the Tribulation (at the three and one half year point), the lawless one will "put an end to sacrifice and offering."

This begins the three and one half year period know as the Great Tribulation or the time of Jacob's trouble, of which Christ said, "If those days had not been cut short, no one would survive" (Matthew 24:22). Christ then returns in judgment, Satan is cast into the bottomless pit for one thousand years and the millennium begins. At the end of the millennium, Satan is loosed "for a season" and he gathers an army against God. This battle of Gog and Magog leads to the Great White Throne judgment and the new heavens and the new earth. Death and Hades will be cast into the lake of fire. Same time period from the point of view of various geographic regions, economic development, political development or special interest. WWII, even in the briefest treatments, covers the same time period of the European and Pacific theaters in different chapters. A detailed history of WWII would cover the same few years from many angles.

Basic Biblical Symbols

Basic Biblical Symbols

This is list of a few Biblical symbols with traditional definitions.

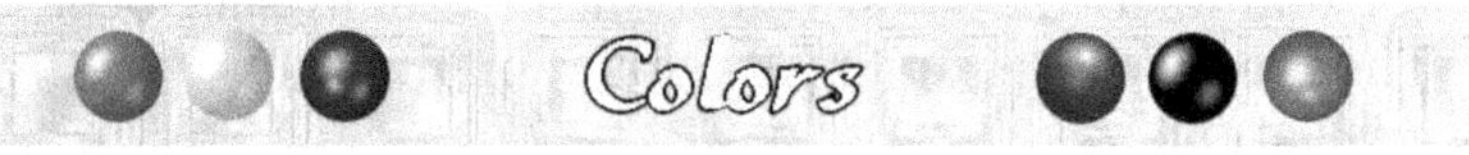

Colors

Red (scarlet, crimson)

1) Sin [Isaiah 1:18—"Come now, let us reason together," says the LORD. "Though your sins are like scarlet, they

shall be as white as snow; though they are red as crimson, they shall be like wool.]

2) Physical life [Lev 17:11—"For the life of a creature is in the blood, and I have given it to you to make atonement for yourselves on the altar; it is the blood that makes atonement for one's life."]

White

1) Purity [Daniel 7:9— "As I looked, thrones were set in place, and the Ancient of Days took his seat. His clothing was as white as snow; the hair of his head was white like wool."]

2) Cleansing [Psalm 51:7— "Cleanse me with hyssop, and I will be clean; wash me, and I will be whiter than snow."]

Purple

1) In the Law, it is always linked with blue and scarlet [e.g., 26:1— "Make the tabernacle with ten curtains of finely twisted linen and blue, purple and scarlet yarn, with cherubim worked into them by a skilled craftsman."]

2) Royalty [Judges 8:26— The weight of the gold rings he asked for came to seventeen hundred shekels, not counting the ornaments, the pendants and the purple garments worn by the kings of Midian or the chains that were on their camels' necks.

Esther 8:15 —Mordecai left the king's presence wearing royal garments of blue and white, a large crown of gold and a purple robe of fine linen. And the city of Susa held a joyous celebration.]

Blue

1) Deity [Exodus 39:30— They made the plate, the sacred diadem, out of pure gold and engraved on it, like an inscription on a seal: HOLY TO THE LORD. 31 Then they fastened a blue cord to it to attach it to the turban, as the LORD commanded Moses.]

2) Spokesman for God [for the true God. Exodus 39:2— They made the ephod of gold, and of blue, purple and scarlet yarn, and of finely twisted linen.

For false gods Ezek 23:5— Oholah engaged in prostitution while she was still mine; and she lusted after her lovers, the Assyrians--warriors 6 clothed in blue, governors and commanders, all of them handsome young men, and mounted horsemen.]

Black

1) Darkness [Deut 4:11— You came near and stood at the foot of the mountain while it blazed with fire to the very heavens, with black clouds and deep darkness.]

2) Divine judgment Ezekiel 30:18— Dark (black) will be the day at Tahpanes when I break the yoke of Egypt; there her proud strength will come to an end.

Green

Life [Gen 1:30—And to all the beasts of the earth and all the birds of the air and all the creatures that move on the ground--everything that has the breath of life in it--I give every green plant for food." And it was so.]

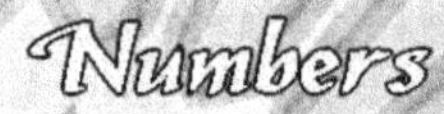

Numbers

One

Unity [GE 2:24 For this reason a man will leave his father and mother and be united to his wife, and they will become one flesh.]

Three

God [1CH 21:10—"Go and tell David, 'This is what the LORD says: "I am giving you three options. Choose one of them for me to carry out against you."""

1CH 21:11— So Gad went to David and said to him, "This is what the LORD says: 'Take your choice: 12 three years of famine, three months of being swept away before your enemies, with their swords overtaking you, or three days of the sword of the LORD--days of plague in the land, with the angel of the LORD ravaging every part of Israel.' Now then, decide how I should answer the one who sent me."]

Six

Man [Exodus 20:8—Remember the Sabbath day by keeping it holy. 9 Six days you shall labor and do all your work, 10 but the seventh day is a Sabbath to the LORD your God. On it you shall not do any work, neither you, nor your son or daughter, nor your manservant or maidservant, nor your animals, nor the alien within your gates. 11 For in six days the LORD made the heavens and the earth, the sea, and all that is in them, but he rested on the seventh day. Therefore the LORD blessed the Sabbath day and made it holy.]

Seven

Perfection or completeness [Pharaoh's dreams (Genesis 41:1 ff– seven cows, seven heads of grain– seven years)

Numbers 23:4 —God met with him, and Balaam said, "I have prepared seven altars, and on each altar I have offered a bull and a ram."

II Kings 5:10– Elisha sent a messenger to say to him, "Go, wash yourself seven times in the Jordan, and your flesh will be restored and you will be cleansed."

Rev 1:4– John, to the seven churches in the province of Asia: Grace and peace to you from him who is, and who was, and who is to come, and from the seven spirits before his throne.]

Ten

God's relationship with the human community [ten commandments, ten plagues]

Jewels

Jewels

Rubies

Extreme value, costly Job 28:18— the price of wisdom is beyond rubies.

Metals

Iron

1) Strength, military might or police power Jeremiah 1:18 — Today I have made you a fortified city, an iron pillar, a bronze wall to stand against the whole land.

2) Some intrinsic value, but less than bronze, silver or gold

3) Not used in the tabernacle or temple

Copper or its alloy Bronze

1) A metal with some intrinsic value, less than silver or gold, but more than iron

2) The metal of which most of the tabernacle and its utensils was made of

3) Strength, but less than iron

4) Symbolic of offering, sacrifice (brazen altar, serpent lifted up in the wilderness)

Silver

1) A metal with intrinsic value, less than gold but much greater than iron or bronze

2) Common money, a coin

3) A few utensils of the tabernacle; many parts of the temple

4) Jewelry

Gold

1) Royalty, deity

2) Intrinsic value above all other metals, often used with silver to mean money or wealth

3) Power, not military but through finances or awe

4) lampstand, altar of incense, mercy seat, ark of the covenant, some utensils

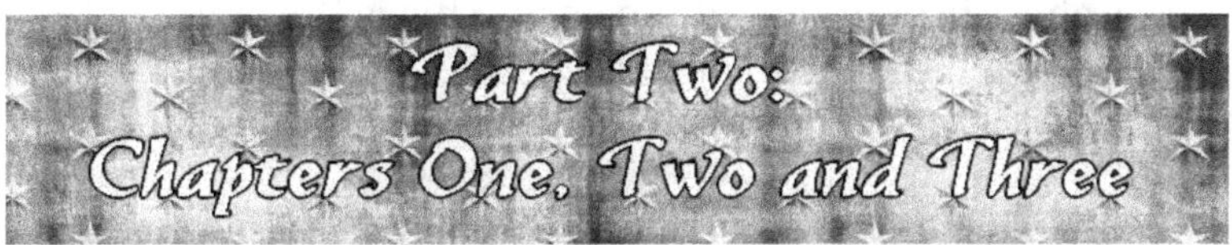

Part Two: Chapters One, Two, and Three

Chapter One

1) The word apocalypse simply means the unveiling, revealing. God did not give us the apocalypse to confuse us, but to make the difficult and obscure clear.

"Soon" is used throughout Revelation to mean what will take place quickly. It does not mean that all the events in Revelation would take place soon after the lifetime of the Apostle John. When the events revealed begin to take place, they will be brought to completion soon. Quickly, speedily or without delay are possible translations.

Also, John had an angel guide him. Chapter 17 has an angel, probably the same one, taking John to a desert and having a conversation with him. Revelation 22:16 ends the book with, "I, Jesus, have sent my angel to give this testimony for the churches." This indicates that the angel remained with John during the entire time.

2) The word for martyr is translated testimony. Throughout Revelation, being a faithful witness often means martyrdom. This statement of John's is a legal formula, what we would call in our courts taking an oath. John is swearing that he faithfully wrote down what he saw.

3) This is the only book in the Word of God which promises a blessing for the reader, the hearer and those

who take to heart what is written. The phrase the time is near closes the book of Revelation in 22:10.

4) The general introduction is over and the specific address is given. John identifies himself as the author and the seven churches of Asia as the recipients. I believe that these 7 churches, at this point, represent all churches throughout all the ages. This is the standard form for a letter. Look at the opening of most of the epistles of the NT and you will see a similar format.

This gives us the basic outline of Revelation: Jesus Christ who is, who was and who is to come. Jesus Christ is alive at the present, Jesus Christ was on this earth historically and He will return to this earth.

Though the exact wording is 'the seven spirits,' the marginal reading of the NIV, the sevenfold spirit is the correct idea. This is God the Holy Spirit, not some lower created being, and He is not divided into 7 parts. This is emphasizing His holiness, completeness and perfection. Notice that these spirits are equal to God the Father and Jesus Christ, and that they are before God's throne. This is the position of both service and power. Throughout Revelation, the throne is the symbol of power, both political and military.

5) I Corinthians 4:2 - It is required that those who have been given a trust must prove faithful. Jesus Christ requires faithfulness and He is the perfect example of what He requires of us. His resurrection guarantees our resurrection. He rules the kings of the earth even when those kings do not acknowledge His existence.

6) The Church of Jesus Christ, every believer, is a kingdom. As priests, we have the responsibility as well as the right to intercede for others. Amen: so be it!

7) Look (KJV behold), He is coming with the clouds. This implies that the clouds are coming with Him, so some have interpreted the clouds to be a host of heavenly beings. The word with can be translated in, though that

would be a weak translation. Probably the best idea is simply that clouds come with Him as He descends. Since this refers to the end of the Great Tribulation, it could refer to the heavenly host, including ourselves, which come with Him. The idea that every eye will see him has a variety of possible interpretations. Since it includes those who pierced Him, probably the best interpretation is that this is a supernatural event where everyone, living or dead, can see Him at the same time. Those who reject Him now will not rejoice to see His day. For unbelievers, this will be a time of mourning as they understand for the first time in their lives their eternal loss.

So shall it be! Amen.

8) The antithesis of America's Established Religion, secular humanism, Jesus states that time had a

beginning and that it will have an end. Uniformitarianism gives unregenerate mankind the confidence to rebel against the God of Glory; a false confidence that they will never be judged for their rebellion. Here Jesus Christ with His own words claims to be God of Eternity and Lord of all time. He again uses the formula for the book of Revelation, who is, and who was, and who is to come. The Almighty is the Greek form of the Hebrew El Shaddai.

9) John explains who he is. He is just a fellow believer, undergoing the same persecutions as all who are obedient to the gospel. He is just a man. The island of Patmos is just West of Ephesus, the southwest coast of Asia Minor, what we know as Turkey. He had been exiled to Patmos because of the word of God and the testimony of Jesus. This was the Roman government attempting to 'shut him up' because they considered John a troublemaker. But God took their evil intentions and used it for his glory.

10) On the Lord's Day means the first day of the week, the day Jesus rose from the dead. This is to distinguish it from the Sabbath. In the Spirit means that what follows is a vision. This is not a dream. It is not vague or unclear: it is just not material. The spiritual world is more real than the material world around us. In II Kings 6:17, when Elisha wanted his servant to see the angelic chariots of fire that surrounded the Syrians, he prayed to the Lord Open his eyes. The book of Revelation is not unclear. It is not a dream subject to various interpretations. It says what it means and means what it says. If we do not understand something in this book, it is not because the book of Revelation is unclear, but our eyes need to be opened.

The word loud occurs in the book of Revelation over 20 times. God is insisting we give him our attention and that no one will be able to say that "we did not have a chance to hear." Usually this loud voice or sound is for believers, but occasionally it will be for everyone on earth.

The word trumpet is the general word for trumpet and does not give us any idea what kind of trumpet.

11) John was commanded to write what he observed. This book is a faithful record of God's Revelation. The seven churches are simply listed in geographic order. That is, Ephesus is the closest to Patmos, Smyrna is the closest to Ephesus, etc. There is no other obvious reason for the order of the churches.

12) Nor is there any special reason for the voice coming from behind John, requiring him to turn around. It is important to realize that John saw lampstands and not candlesticks (KJV). The oil flowing to the lamps is a symbol of the Holy Spirit throughout Scripture. The contrast, when it is made, with a lamp and any other kind of illumination (candle, torch, etc.) is the source of power. This is a constant reminder to us: Whatever we do, is it of God or is it of ourselves?

13) The lampstand of the tabernacle (Exodus 25), and the temple, was only one lampstand, though it had 7 branches with seven lamps. These are individual lampstands and Jesus Christ is among them; each lamp represents one of the seven churches this book in addressed to (v 20 The seven lampstands are the seven churches.)

The phrase "like a son of man" comes from Daniel 7:13. Though God uses it frequently for Ezekiel and Daniel, in this passage it is obviously referring to God Himself. It was Christ Jesus' favorite term for Himself. The robe to the feet shows modesty and that He is at rest (physical labor is difficult with this much clothing). His very garments proclaim the glory and majesty of God.

The word translated sash is usually translated belt or since it was hollow and could carry money, purse. Since Christ had this belt made of gold around His chest, this is the symbol of royalty or military victory. This was a common symbol in the ancient world.

14) Compare this vision of Christ to the man Daniel saw in Daniel 10:5,6. But here in Revelation the appearance of Jesus Christ was like that of the Ancient of Days in Daniel 7:9. White is not only the symbol of purity, but also the symbol of glory.

His eyes are blazing fire and this is for His Church, the seven churches. Fire purifies, cleanses and judges. In Luke 16:24, this word blazing means the fires of hell. It always means some form of judgment and intensifies the normal word for fire.

15) The feet of the four living creatures in Ezekiel's vision (Ezekiel 1) also glowed like burnished bronze. The man who showed Ezekiel the new temple in Ezekiel 40 was entirely of bronze. The legs of the man in Daniel 10:6 were of burnished bronze. Israel will be given hoofs of bronze (Micah 4:13) to break to pieces many nations. The man in Daniel 10:6 also had a voice which had the sound of a multitude.

16) From the star of Bethlehem to here this is the normal word for star. We would have no reason to believe that it had any other meaning exempt that Jesus explains that the seven stars are angels of the seven churches. (v. 20) They are in His right hand of power and protection. We can infer from this that every local congregation throughout the Church age has a 'guardian angel'. While Jesus Christ has promised us as individuals never to leave us or forsake us, I do not know of any passage of Scripture that promises individual believers of a guardian angel.

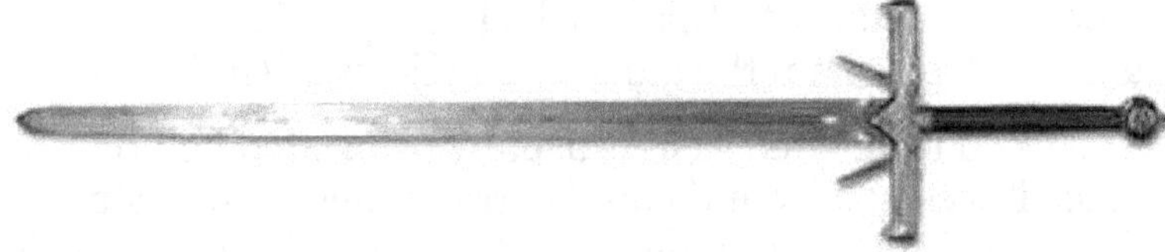

The sword of the Spirit is the Word of God (Ephesians 6:17). The word of God is sharper than any two-edged sword (Hebrews 4:12). This sword out of His mouth will be the final destruction of the wicked who continue to rebel at the end of the Great Tribulation (Revelation 19:15 & 21).

The man Daniel saw (10:6) had a face like lightning. This is the glory of God.

17) Daniel had his face to the ground and was in a deep sleep (8:18) at the vision of God. John fell at his feet as though dead. Those who take the things of God lightly believe another gospel. For those who are faithful and true, Jesus will provide the necessary strength.

The recurring phrase First and the Last, Alpha and Omega affirm that God created this world, that He has the right and that He will judge and bring this world to an end.

18) The gospel is the death, burial and resurrection of Jesus Christ according to the Scriptures. Death is not just the death of the body, but the eternal separation from God. Hades is the judgment for willful rebellion against a thrice- holy God. The obedience of Jesus Christ gives Him eternal life, the power to give others that same eternal life and the need to judge those who reject Him.

19) John is commissioned by the Lord Jesus Christ to write 1) what he has seen 2) what he is seeing 3) what will take place later. This is the outline of Revelation: History prior to the Church Age, The Church Age, the future (Tribulation, Judgment, Millennium, Great White Throne Judgment, New Heavens and New Earth).

20) This is how the word mystery is used throughout the Word of God: something that we do not know and cannot know is divinely revealed to use. It is no longer hidden after God explains it to us.

Chapter Two

There are many interpretations of the letter(s?) to the seven Churches. I believe that the entire book of Revelation is the letter and that each Church had a special message just for that congregation. The letter was first given to the Ephesian Church, then to the Church located at Smyrna, etc., ending with the Church in Laodicea. Each Church had the opportunity to see what was written to the others.

Among conservative, fundamentalist believers there are many, perhaps even most, who believe that these seven Churches represent a timeline of the Church Age. I do not believe that because a serious examination of the Church Age does not fit into 7 separate time periods. As an example, more believers have been martyred for Jesus Christ since World War II than all of the history of the Church prior to this time. Western Churches do not talk about this much because our brothers and sisters in Christ who are giving their lives for Him are in Communist countries such as China, Vietnam, Korea and the Soviet Union; Islamic countries such as Afghanistan, Pakistan, Indonesia, Iraq and Iran; Third World countries such as sub-Saharan Africa, interiors of Brazil, Columbia and Venezuela. But the persecuted Church is Smyrna, the 2nd Church in the order given in Revelation. And even though the Church of Jesus Christ in America and Western Europe is primarily Laodicean since WWII, the Western European church of the late middle ages was just as lukewarm as we are. Also, every commentator wants to make the age he lives in the Laodicean Church. Commentators during the Reformation period obviously make a different timeline from twentieth century commentators. Whose timeline is accurate? I have never seen two alike.

The examples can continue, but I believe that the primary reason that Christians today want to view this letter to the seven Churches as a timeline of the Church Age is to weaken their responsibility to the warnings. If the letter to the Ephesian church is the Apostolic Church (primarily) then we do not need to pay as close attention to the warnings. I see, however, no reason to believe that every warning to each church can apply to every church today. He who has an ear, let him hear what the Spirit says to the churches.

1) The word angel can also mean messenger. Some think that this means the pastor or elder. I believe that this is teaching that each of these Churches has a guardian angel, an angel who works with the Holy Spirit and the elder of each congregation. Ephesus was John's 'home church.' He lived there for decades before his exile to Patmos. It was the largest city of these seven churches, a seaport in southwest Turkey. Each of these messages was dictated to John word for word by Jesus Christ. Combined, these seven messages are the longest message Jesus gave to His churches recorded anywhere in the Word of God.

To support my basic position about the nature of these seven messages, all of the Churches could see all of the characteristics of Jesus Christ that John records in chapter one. Each church, however, has one or two things emphasized. First there is an emphasis of something about Christ Jesus. Next there is a commendation, followed by condemnation, closing with a promise and/or a warning.

Ephesus saw Jesus Christ as holding the seven stars in his right hand and walking among the seven golden lampstands. Seven here is the number of completeness. The right hand is power and authority. Jesus is emphasizing His complete power and control over His church, even over our guardian angel. It is also the love and protection of the right hand. The right hand is the hand of favor. Since each individual Church is a lampstand, Jesus is emphasizing His personal presence in and among the churches. Again this emphasizes His power, control, protection and presence.

The Ephesian Church has more words of commendation than any other Church. Since she was larger and more influential than any of these other Churches, this is what we would expect. These are not just superficial, shallow comments either. Jesus Christ knows her deeds. The commendation for each Church begins with I know. The first time in the Word of God this phrase is found is Genesis 4:1, which the NIV translates Adam lay with his wife Eve. The KJV more literally translates Adam knew Eve his wife.

The closest experience we can have to the way God know us is sexual intercourse. Jesus knows us completely and intimately. So each of the things Ephesus is commended for is something that Jesus loves about Ephesus and that Jesus has an intimate knowledge and experience of. Deeds, hard work, perseverance, intolerance of wicked men, testing men's spiritual claims, persevering and enduring hardships without growing weary are all works which Jesus loves and desires to see in all of His churches. May this commendation be said of our church!

This is not the standard of the world. This world wants us to tolerate wickedness, to allow wickedness in without any standards to measure it against, no tests. Satan wants us to grow weary and give up our standards.

4) In I Corinthians 13 Paul tells us that if we do not have love, we are nothing. Even if we are doing all of the right things, we are nothing without love. Jesus said that the first and greatest commandment was to love the Lord our God with all of our heart, soul, mind and strength. The Ephesian Church was doing everything right, but while doing right, had left her first love, Jesus Christ. The word for left is sometimes translated abandon, desert or divorce. Doing the service became more important than the One being served. Remember Mary and Martha, keeping in mind the words of Christ, You should have practiced the latter, without neglecting the former. (Matthew 23:23 and Luke 11:42)

5) Leaving our first love, Jesus Christ, is a sin of which we must repent. It seems odd after this list of works for which the Ephesian church is commended, that for repentance they are commanded to do the things you did at first. In the book of Acts we are told that the early Ephesians held the Lord Jesus Christ in high honor, that they turned from evil, they burned books of sorcery, that Paul daily taught in the school of Tyrannus for two years and that God worked mightily through Paul healing the sick. At Ephesus Aquilla and Priscilla taught Apollos about Christ, since he only knew John's baptism. At Ephesus Paul baptized believers who only knew of John's baptism into the name of Christ and these believers spoke in tongues and prophesied. In the letter to the Ephesians, Paul writes that this church is largely a gentile church. They seem to need to be grounded in the Word of God.

The Ephesian church no longer loved God with all of their heart, soul, mind and strength. They were no longer searching the Scriptures daily and living in obedience to the things the Spirit of God revealed to them through the Word of God. This departure from our first love is a fall from a great height. The threatened judgment of God is the removal of their lampstand. The lampstand is both the witness in the community and the very existence as a church.

6) Why is the praise of the hatred of the works, practices, deeds of the Nicolaitans listed after the warning and not with the rest of the commendations? We do not know exactly what the doctrines of the Nicolaitans were. I believe that the Nicolaitans symbolize all heresy, all false doctrine. In this one area, the Ephesians had not left their first love. I believe that this hatred of false teaching is a work of love for Christ.

7) He who has an ear, let him hear what the Spirit says to the churches. These exact words are repeated at the end of each message to each Church. Every believer and every church has the physical ability to hear the message of Jesus Christ. God has given us the message of His Word, and along with that message the responsibility to hear, listen and understand that message. That is our responsibility, which we cannot claim before the judgment bar of God that we did not know about. It is also interesting that the message to hear is addressed, all seven times, to the churches.

The promise of the right to eat from the tree of life, which is in the paradise of God, is part of salvation. All who are saved have the right to eat from the tree of life. What this warning is saying, and it is the same as the warning given to six of the seven churches, is that not everyone who is a member of a church is actually saved. The emphasis for the Ephesians on the tree of life in the paradise of God is rest, which is the reward for faithful service.

8) The name Smyrna means myrrh. It was a city 40 miles north of Ephesus. The emphasis on Jesus Christ is that He is the First and the Last, who died and came to life again. He is the creator and judge of all things. He gives

life to all and will take that life back for those who reject Him. His resurrection not only gives Him eternal life, but also gives Him the right to give that life to others.

9) The same knowledge Jesus has of the Ephesian church, He has for each church. Once more, the spiritual view of a situation is the real situation. Persecution, affliction and material poverty hide the true riches of the Smyrnan church. Do not make the mistake of thinking that all who are materially poor are spiritually rich. The vast majority of the materially poor are also spiritually poor. It is sad that material wealth usually means spiritual poverty. Smyrna's riches were a result of her love for her Lord and her obedience to His word.

This, along with Paul's letter to the Galatians, is the clearest statement in Scripture that those who are physical Jews but reject Jesus Christ are not truly Jews. In Smyrna, their attack of the church earned them the title of Synagogue of Satan.

10) Smyrna was promised suffering, imprisonment and persecution for ten days. Whether this means ten actual days as we would count days or this is symbolic is unclear: That the early church suffered tremendous persecution is well documented.

The crown of life is not eternal salvation. That is promised to all who believe, whether they are martyred or not. This is a special reward just for those who are faithful unto death. This crown, is reward given to a winner in an athletic contest or to a victorious general.

11) The overcomer will not be hurt at all by the second death. This promise of comfort for steadfast faithfulness is for anyone in the Church Age. This is not salvation by works, but, the faith that saves, works. By their fruit you will know them. God is looking on the heart.

12) The word Pergamum means height or elevation. The emphasis on Jesus Christ is the sharp two-edged sword. This sword is an offensive weapon, not some symbol of judgment on the church. It is the Word of God by which the church can triumph.

What Jesus knows about Pergamum is that they live where Satan has his throne. Since Satan is not omnipotent, he must be in one place at a time. His throne is on earth, though it can move from place to place. To oppose the very throne of Satan is a privilege, a responsibility and a challenge. This is a tremendous commendation to remain faithful, even unto death.

14-16) Even in this steadfastness, however, some in the church have embraced heresies. Failure to repent of these heresies will cause the sword of the Spirit to become not the offensive weapon it is intended to be, but an instrument of judgment within the church.

17) The message of warning is to sift true believers from unbelievers. The hidden manna and the white stone with a new name ... known only to him who receives it is for true believers only.

18) Thyatira was known for manufacturing purple dye, the color of royalty. The emphasis of Jesus Christ is on judgment, purification, cleansing and purging.

19) John writes that Jesus knows that, in contrast to the Ephesian church, they have more love and more deeds now than at the first.

20) Thyatira was a tolerant church. While America's Established Religion holds tolerance up as a supreme virtue, God condemns toleration of evil as a sign of unbelief. The Jerusalem Council in Acts 15 wanted to place as little burden on the new gentile believers as

possible, so they only required that abstain from sexual immorality, things offered to idols, things strangled and blood. A woman in Thyatira claiming to be a prophetess was enticing those in the church of Thyatira into the sins of sexual immorality and the eating of food sacrificed to idols. In Galatians 1 Paul said that though we or an angel from heaven should preach any other gospel, let them be accursed (damned).

21) Jesus himself says that Jezebel was unwilling to repent.

22-23) Therefore, she and those who commit adultery with her will suffer intensely, unless they repent of her ways. Adultery here is both sexual immorality and idolatry. Judgment is in this life, which includes intense personal, physical suffering and the death of her children. Jesus will make their sin and judgments obvious to all. I will repay each of you according to your deeds.

24) Not everyone in Thyatira had followed Jezebel. The deep things of Satan are really only so-called deep secrets.

25) Those who have not followed after Jezebel and the so-called deep secrets of Satan are simply commanded to hold on to what you have until I come. I believe that this is referring to Christ's immediate judgment on Jezebel, not the rapture of the entire church. This should encourage us in our struggle against sin.

26-28) Again, the promise to rule is given to all believers. Those who do not receive this authority are not true believers. The phrase morning star is not in the vision of Christ Jesus in chapter 1. It emphasizes the dawning of truth and the judgment of sin.

Chapter Three

1) The word "Sardis" means "red ones." Sardis was the capital city of Lydia and known as a luxurious city. The emphasis on Jesus Christ is that He holds the seven spirits of God and the seven stars. The number seven is completeness and perfection. He is the standard by which all things are measured as well as the finished, completed work of God. The spirits of God and the stars are means through which God communicates to and empowers His church. Though the Word of God is standard by which we judge everything, God's spirit still directs us in our daily walk. The emphasis on He holds the spirits and stars says that He controls them. Sardis was a church which was not controlled by the Spirit of God and did not allow her guardian angel to protect her.

Jesus knew her works, as He knows our works. Unlike Ephesus, Smyrna, Pergamum or Thyatira, no specific work is mentioned. The implication is that none of the works of the church of Sardis was acceptable in God's sight. You have reputation (literally name of or for life) for being alive, but you are dead. They claimed the name of Christ outwardly, but they were spiritually dead.

2) It is obvious that most of the people in the church of Sardis were unsaved, but not everyone. The unsaved had suppressed Biblical doctrine and practices. But what remained was so weak that it was about to die. The deed which Sardis needed was repentance unto salvation.

3) They had the truth. The call was to wake up! Listen and obey! Why should we think that we are better than the church in Sardis? Failure to wake up would not only result in judgment, but that they would be unaware of the judgment.

4) The only commendation, the only praise for the church of Sardis is that there are some true believers even in Sardis. True salvation washes our garments white in the blood of the lamb. Soiled garments are stained with the sins of this world and will not permit us into heaven.

5) The phrase blot out his name from the book of life bothers many because it does not seem to line up with the rest of the teachings of Scripture about eternal security. The best explanation that I know of is that Christ's atonement is sufficient for all men throughout all time. Because of Christ's atonement, everyone's name is written in the lamb's book of life. At the point of death, anyone who dies still rejecting Jesus Christ will, at that moment, have his name blotted out of the book of life. This is the only place in the Word of God where this word is used this way.

7) The word Philadelphia simply means brotherly love. It is interesting that the characteristics of Jesus Christ which are emphasized for the Philadelphian church are characteristics which are not mentioned in Chapter 1. Holy and true are basic characteristics of God which no other spiritual being can claim. These characteristics cause believers to rejoice and praise Him, but rebels to

mourn because when their wickedness confronts His holiness, their doom is sealed.

The key of David is mentioned nowhere else in the Bible. The word translated key is only found six times. The other five are: Matthew 16:10 the keys to the kingdom, Luke 11:52 the key to knowledge, Revelation 1:18 I hold the keys to death and Hades, Revelation 9:1 The star was given the key to the shaft of the Abyss, Revelation 20:1 I saw an angel coming down out of heaven, having the key to the Abyss and holding in his hand a great chain.

Ezekiel 37:25 And David my servant will be their prince forever. There is some question as to whether this is the Millennium or the new heavens and the new earth. It is, however, a very common theme throughout the Old Testament. Remember that Ezekiel wrote this during the Babylonian captivity, about 500 years after the death of David the King.

So the key of David is the authority to rule, a promise given to all believers. The opening and shutting authority is for the Church Age. The Philadelphian church is called the great missionary church since Jesus opens and closes doors for her. Believers today use the idea that the great Philadelphian age is over as an excuse for lazy indolence. We do not attempt great things for God and then claim that we do not live in the Philadelphian church. The Philadelphian church can be any church in any time, if we are willing to be obedient as they were.

8) As with Sardis, Jesus said I know your deeds. Unlike Sardis, Jesus is pleased with the deeds of Philadelphia. Yes, they only have little strength, like all of us. Yet they used all that they had for His glory and He blessed it.

9) As in Smyrna, the phrase synagogue of Satan occurs again. Those who claim to be Jews outwardly but rebel against the Word of God are of the synagogue of Satan. As Paul condemned them harshly, so Jesus with His own mouth calls them liars.

10) This promise to be kept from the Great Tribulation is given to all believers. Once again, Jesus is saying that there might be unbelievers hiding even in great Philadelphian church.

11) The loss Jesus talks about is crowns, the rewards for obedience. Even faithful believers can lose their rewards through sin.

12) Here is a list of promises of permanent blessings for righteous believers. No one here on earth can fully comprehend what this fully means. We can be certain that nothing here on earth can compare.

13) God wants us to listen to and remember His blessings, as well as His warnings.

14) Laodicea means "justice of the people". The city of Laodicea was near Colosse.

Every commentator that I know who believes that chapters 2 and 3 are a timeline of the Church Age, whether an early church father, a reformer or a modern scholar, believe that their own generation is the Laodicean church. What a testimony to human depravity!

Since I do not believe that these churches represent a timeline, I can say that probably each and every commentator was right!

All three emphases of Christ Jesus, the Amen, the faithful and true witness, the ruler of God's creation, show Him to be not only the ruler of the spirit world and the future judge and ruler, but the ruler of this present world according to eternal truth which does not change. Jesus Christ is ruling now according to His word, which does not change.

15-16) One last time Jesus Christ says, I know your deeds. The temperatures hot and cold mean fervently for the truth (hot) or frigid towards the truth. This is the apathetic church. It does not necessarily mean that they are apathetic towards everything, just that they are apathetic towards Jesus Christ and His Word. Being spit out of Christ's mouth is more than just a loss of rewards. It is complete judgment. It means the fires of hell.

17) These people love the world, as John in his first letter told them not to (2:15). The love of the father is not in them. They see their material wealth and do not understand their true condition. They are wholly given over to idolatry, and do not even realize it. They do not understand that they are completely destitute (nothing to offer Christ), without salvation (the white robes of Christ's righteousness) and spiritually blind (unable to see their true condition).

18) Christ offers remedies for each of these conditions: gold (His royalty, deity and wealth), white clothes (His righteousness), eye salve (His healing of our understanding through His spirit).

19) What makes the Laodiceans a Church? Jesus loves them and asks them to repent. They are being rebuked

and disciplined in this life, to the end of avoiding eternal punishment.

20) This verse has been used for centuries as a salvation call to unbelievers. I stand at the door and knock. Others point out that this is an invitation to a specific church to

repent. I believe that it is both. Christ is not outside of a true believer knocking to come in. Yet Jesus Himself calls this His church. The invitation to eat is an invitation not only to the most intimate fellowship, but to become like Him through dining with Him. He is waiting for our invitation. He will not force Himself on us.

21) To him who overcomes, I will give the right to sit with me on my throne, just as I overcame and sat down with my Father on his throne. If this promise can be given to the Laodicean church, then it can be applied to anyone who is willing to repent.

22) A final call to listen and obey.

Part Three: Chapters Four and Five

Part Three: Chapters Four and Five

Chapter Four

1-2) After this I looked: The Lord Jesus Christ stopped speaking; the letter to the seven churches was completed. These seven messages were given to John one right after the other, taking only a matter of minutes. After the Lord Jesus Christ stopped speaking, John looked around. He saw a door open in heaven. This is very clearly a vision, as explained in 1:10. John is still in the spirit at this time. We will be in the spirit throughout the book of Revelation.

This is the rapture of the Church and the end of the Church Age. The open door leads to heaven and John represents the Church. The voice like a trumpet commands John to go to heaven. The rapture will be at the trump of God.

Jesus Christ Himself told John that He would show him what must take place after this. Everything in the book of Revelation from this point on takes place after the rapture. Since John went with the saints, the first thing we as saints will see after the rapture will be a throne in heaven.

3) The one sitting on the throne is similar to the one sitting on the throne in the vision of Ezekiel. I believe that vision of Ezekiel is the same throne that John saw,

though at different times. Ezekiel looked from under the expanse, John was on the top of the crystal sea.

The rainbow is God's promise to the entire earth. It is not only a promise not to destroy the entire earth with a flood, but it is the sign of the everlasting covenant; God has given to us as food everything that moves. We are not to eat blood and whoever sheds the blood of man, by man shall his blood be shed. (Genesis 9:6)

4) The usual conservative interpretation is that the twenty-four thrones represent both the church and Israel, the twelve tribes of Israel and the twelve apostles. This is in fulfillment of Jesus' prophecy that many would come ... and ... take their places with Abraham, Isaac and Jacob in the kingdom of heaven. (Matthew 8:11)

Dressed in white means they are clothed in Christ's righteousness. The crowns, on their heads are the rewards for the deeds in this life.

5) The flashes of lightning, rumblings and peals of thunder coming from the throne show God's power and imminent use of that power. Here the seven lamps represent the sevenfold spirit of God, not the churches. The blazing lamps are the power of God's Spirit, to judge, purify, cleanse, reveal, illuminate and test. For believers,

this is the judgment seat of Christ, the handing out of rewards.

6) I believe that this sea of crystal is what Ezekiel saw as an expanse above him. This is the 'dividing line,' if you will, between heaven and earth. Though heaven can, if they so desire, view the material world, the material world cannot view heaven unless God miraculously opens someone's eyes. The clear sea also represents God's purity and holiness.

As in Ezekiel's vision, there are four living creatures. Ezekiel's creatures had wheels covered with eyes. John's creatures are covered with eyes, in front and in back. Jesus said about the eye, The eye is the lamp of the body (Matthew 6:22). Ezekiel saw his vision when Judah was judged by the Babylonian captivity. John's vision is the judgment seat of Christ for believers. The eyes represent God seeing and knowing everything about us, not only our deeds but also our motives. The Word of God judges the thoughts and attitudes (intents KJV) of the heart (Hebrews 4:12).

7) Each creature in Ezekiel's vision had four faces; a man, a lion, an ox and an eagle. In John's vision each creature had one face but there are four different faces; a lion, an ox, a man and an eagle. Each of the four gospels has a different emphasis of Christ. In Matthew He is the son of David (lion of the tribe of Judah). In Mark He is the sacrificial servant (ox of the burnt offering). Luke portrays Him as the son of man (man of sorrows and acquainted with grief). In John He is the Son of God (ruler of the air and victorious over the serpent). The order of these creatures in revelation is the same as the order of the gospels: lion, ox, man, eagle.

8) Ezekiel identified the creatures he saw in chapter 10 as cherubim. The creatures John sees act like the seraphs of Isaiah's vision (Isaiah 6). Each creature has six wings, as do the seraphs. Their eyes are emphasized again: they

know the thoughts and motives of believers and unbelievers alike. This is our period of examination.

Like the seraphs in Isaiah's vision these creatures say Holy, holy, holy is the Lord God Almighty. They change the message of the seraphs to finish their praise with the theme of Revelation, who was, and is, and is to come.

9) The only way these living creatures can give glory, honor and thanks is by what they say and what they do. The word o{tan is almost always translated when. I feel that this should be translated 'when' here. I believe that the laying down of the crowns is a one-time act, not something repeated over and over. Since the living creatures never stop saying holy, holy, holy is the Lord God Almighty, this giving glory, honor and thanks must be something different. We do not know exactly what John means, because he did not write it down, but when we are in heaven and see it ourselves, we will know exactly what giving glory, honor and thanks means.

The one sitting on the throne is God the Father. The emphasis here is that God lives forever and ever. Jesus Christ is the one who is, was and is to come. God the Father lives forever and ever. For us both phrases mean the same thing. God created the world, the world is temporary and the world will be judged and brought to an end.

10) Once again, the twenty-four elders represent both the church and Israel (or all Old Testament believers). Our joy and privilege will be to fall down before him who sits on the throne, and worship him who lives forever and ever. The idea of worship is both the bodily position of kneeling or lying down and the attitude of submission. The constant emphasis on phrases such as lives forever and ever is that God and heaven are real and eternal. This life is a vapor, a mist and passing away. The entire purpose of this life is to earn crowns that we may them lay at the feet of him who lives forever and ever.

11) There we will praise and worship Him. He is worthy of our praise by right of creation. Everything exists because of

him. This is the foundation of America's established religion, secular humanism. It needs evolution to deny God's right to receive glory and honor and power. It does that by denying that God is the creator. The foundational truth which they deny is that everything exists because of the will of God.

Chapter Five

1) The phrase then I saw indicates that this scene in heaven happens after the events in chapter 4. Verse one of chapter 4 symbolizes the Rapture, and the end of verse ten shows the twenty-four elders laying their crowns before the throne. We receive our crowns at the judgment seat of Christ, so verse ten must be after the judgment seat of Christ for believers. None of the judgments called the Great Tribulation have begun yet. We are not given any time reference to events on earth. From the point of view of someone left behind on earth, the judgment seat of Christ might take place in seconds, it might take years or it might take days or months. The Word of God does not say. The only Scriptural indication is the phrase then I saw at the beginning of this chapter. We do not even know how long the time period is between the Rapture and the beginning of the seventieth week of Daniel, that is, the covenant which allows the restarting of animal sacrifices in the temple.

The right hand is power, control, and authority, as is sitting on a throne. This is the ultimate authority to judge the universe and those in it.

A sealed scroll was common throughout the Roman and non-Roman worlds. Property deeds, business transactions, wills, commands to officers and public records were all sealed. Many scrolls could, upon penalty of death in Roman law, only be opened by the one intended to read the contents of the scroll. The number of seals, seven, is the number of completion and perfection. Many times throughout the Word of God, God says that an individual, family or nation was not yet ready for judgment. Seven (the number of completion or perfection) seals says that the earth is ready for the final judgment. Multiple seals allow for a scroll to be partially unrolled to read something for one person or at one time that needed to wait for either someone else or a later time. It also can mean that more than one person seals the scroll. Seven seals would then mean that the scroll was sealed, perfectly and completely, by the sevenfold spirit of God.

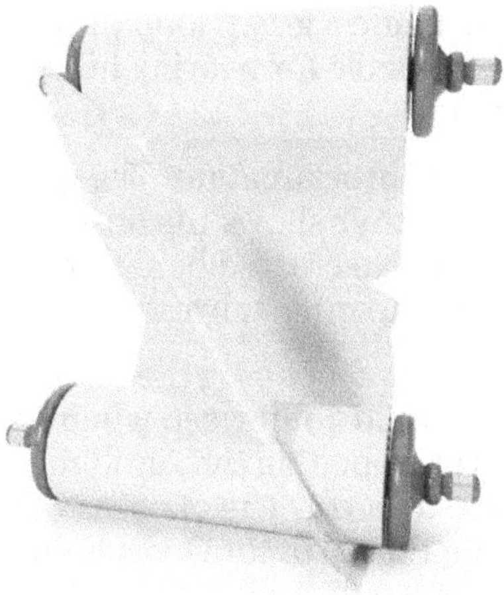

The writing on both sides might be another way of saying that the sins are filled up. A similar image of a cup filling up is given in Genesis 15:16, the iniquity of the Amorites is not yet full. There is no room left for any more iniquity; judgment will come quickly.

The phrase with writing on both sides probably means, though, the Word of God. Forever, oh Lord, thy Word is settled in heaven. When the seals which keep the thrice-holy God separate from this world are broken and the holiness of God comes down to earth, sin will be judged, for God cannot dwell in the presence of sin.

Another possible interpretation is that the writing on both sides is a record of human deeds. Since all our righteous acts are like filthy rags (Isaiah 64:6), I see this interpretation being another view of our sins filling up the scrolls.

Whatever the exact writing is, for believers it means salvation and redemption; for unbelievers it means judgment and eternal damnation.

2-3) The angel John saw was strong, mighty, powerful, and forceful. He made a great, loud proclamation. Everyone is responsible for hearing him. The angel is proclaiming, not

making a one-time proclamation. The question he is asking, Who is worthy? shows the absolute lost condition of the human race. No created being, spiritual or material, is worthy to offer salvation to the human race.

Breaking the seals and opening the scrolls means judgment. Why would John weep when no one was able to judge the earth? Opening the scroll means bringing the Word of God to earth. The opening of the seven seals means preparing the earth for God's holiness, bringing God's kingdom to earth, which means judgment of sin.

The emphasis in the Word of God is not on what the scroll contains, but on the worthiness of the one to open the scroll. In the Roman world, the contents of a sealed scroll were unknown to the one opening it. But it was the responsibility of the one receiving the scroll to open it and obey it.

In heaven are the angels, redeemed souls of mankind, and the heavenly host which would include beings we cannot imagine and God Himself. God is limited by His attributes. He cannot violate His holiness, His righteousness, His justice. He cannot look on evil (Habakkuk 1:13). On earth are all the material creatures known to man. Under the earth are the demons of hell, the departed spirits of the damned, the angels which kept not their first estate (Jude 6) and possibly the creatures of the pit which are neither angels nor demons.

Could means to be able, or have the power to do something. The root form of this word is the basis for dynamite. Unworthy to open the scroll means unable to open the scroll. Verse three ends with or even look inside it.

Opening the scroll means owning the rights to the scroll. Those unworthy to open the scroll cannot even find out what the scroll has written on it.

4) The only reason I can understand for John weeping when no one was found worthy to open the scroll was that he understood that this scroll was the earth's redemption. We accept redemption by faith as of a little child. We are unable to grasp what redemption truly is. But we know that without it we are lost and John represents the hopelessness of mankind without redemption.

5) An elder instructs John that redemption is provided. He emphasizes two aspects of Jesus Christ which give Him the right to break the seals, open the scroll and read what is inside. Jesus is the Lion of the tribe of Judah, as prophesied by Jacob in Genesis 49. Royal, regal, triumphant, is a lion among beasts; Judah is the line of the Messiah. The Root of David means the offspring

which would rule like David; heir to the Davidic promises.

6) The creature, which the elder introduced to John as a triumphant Lion, looked like a slain Lamb standing in the center of the throne. The way He triumphed was to lay down His life as a sacrificial lamb. His death was His means of victory. The living lamb looking as it had been slain is a favorite image of Christ for artists throughout the history of the Church. Standing in the center of the throne is the ultimate position of power. The four living creatures and the elders encircle him. These creatures and the elders represent all of redeemed creation worshiping the Lamb. Seven represents perfection or completeness; the seven horns represent perfect, complete power, the power to force someone to behave a certain way. Horns on beasts in visions throughout the Old Testament represent the power to force people to behave a certain way; police power, taxation, courts, favors for obedience, and finally if all other forms of coercion fail, military power.

Here seven eyes represent the spirit of God. The work of the Spirit of God for His Church is complete because the Church has been raptured. The perfect Spirit of God has completed His work of going out into all the earth. His knowledge of all, including our attitudes and deeds, is perfect and complete. Isaiah listed seven spirits the Messiah would have (Isaiah 11:1-3): wisdom, understanding, counsel, might, knowledge, the fear of the Lord, quick understanding in the fear of the Lord (KJV).

7) The throne was probably quite large, so the Father, sitting on the throne and the son, standing in the center of the throne would not be in the same place at the same time. There is no description of the throne in Scripture. The son takes the scroll from the right hand of the Father. This is the transfer of the power to rule creation from the father to the son.

8) When the Son takes the scroll from the right hand of the Father, all creation praises Him and our representatives worship Him. Does a harp mean only a harp, all stringed instruments or does it mean all forms of music? Whatever it means, we will be praising God with music. The only other articles of worship at this time are golden bowls full of incense, which are the prayers of the saints. All of the saints at this time are in heaven. Are these the prayers we are offering now, which are used again at this moment? Are these the prayers of the tribulation saints? Do we still pray in heaven and these are our future prayers?

Since this is the moment of our redemption and the beginning of the earth's redemption, this is a time for praise and worship. We will desire those we love who are left behind to repent, but this is the ultimate fulfillment of Christ's model prayer Thy Kingdom come. For those who love His appearing, this will be the acceptance of a lifetime of prayers.

9) This is not a time of weeping. This is our redemption! With hearts overflowing with joy we praise God in a doxology of redemption. This is praise of redemption complete (for believers). These words have been used in everything from simple one-line melodies to the complex polyphonies of Handel's Messiah. But Christ said that He will make all things new. New because we will have our redeemed bodies and eternal life. We sing of a hope yet unrealized. In heaven this will be a triumphant praise.

We begin by boldly proclaiming that He is worthy. He is worthy to redeem mankind. He is worthy to judge sin. He is worthy because He died on the cross, the perfect redemption for our sin. He is worthy because He shed His blood. He is worthy because His sacrifice once for all was sufficient for all, for all time.

10) Because of His sacrifice, we are a kingdom and priests. This is not to puff us up with pride, but to show our status, that we serve our God. How do we serve Him?

By reigning on the earth. We will return with Him at the end of the Great Tribulation. But at this time, we praise Him in heaven.

11) Now John sees innumerable angels. We do not know where they were before this, but we know that they arrive just after the elders (representing us) and the living creatures finish singing the new song. Also this teaches us that the living creatures are not angels.

12) The encircling angels, however, do not sing their praise; they only say it.

As the elders and 4 living creatures began, so the angels begin by loudly proclaiming that He is worthy! Jesus Christ, the willing sacrifice, is worthy to receive the blessings of the sevenfold Spirit: power and wealth and wisdom and strength and honor and glory and praise.

13) The phrase all creatures means exactly that: all created beings. This is a different word from the four living creatures. That could just as easily be translated living ones, or living beings or living beasts. It is actually just the word living in a form which means creatures, or beings, etc.

The interpretations for all creatures range from everything that ever was created, including Satan, demons, fallen angels, those now in hell to people who believe that this just means creatures alive at this time (animals and people on earth). This is an issue which I must leave in God's sovereign control and confess that I do not know. As with the angels, these creatures are not singing, but saying.

People who believe that evil spirits join in saying this see a 'forced praise' that is not genuine. They see this as the time that every knee shall bow (Romans 14:11, Philippians 2:10). Though possible, I see this as genuine praise. As we shall see as we progress through Revelation, the Greek concept of "all" does not always mean 100% like we do. I do not believe that evil spirits or rebellious men join in this praise.

This praise is directed to the Father as well as the Son. This is a fourfold doxology, into the ages of the ages (forever and ever).

14) The living creatures say amen (so be it) to these doxologies and they, together with the elders, fall down in worship. They put their stamp of approval on all of the doxologies. This ends the period of praise and the Lamb is ready to begin the process of purifying the earth.

Part Four: Chapters Six-Eight

Part Four: Chapters Six-Eight

Chapter Six

1) This is the next major transition: I watched as the Lamb... John is still in heaven, the same place where he was at the end of chapter 5. The elders, representing all believers throughout all the ages, have laid their crowns at the feet of him who sits on the throne (4:10). The Lamb is worthy to open the scroll and it is time to open the scroll. When the first seal is opened, one of the living creatures says, "Come." The Scriptures do not tell us which of the living creatures spoke. It does not matter. They are equal. I believe that as the seven lamps are a sevenfold representation of the Spirit of God, the four living creatures are a fourfold representation of Christ himself. Each one has a different emphasis. While Christ Himself is worshiped, He leads the redeemed of all the ages as our great high priest in the worship of the Father.

The voice like thunder not only grabbed attention, but also made everyone who heard responsible. "Come!" is not a polite request, but a military command. John, representing the entire Church, had the responsibility to observe and understand what God would do next.

2) John obeyed and observed: "I looked. Behold! A white horse!" White represents purity, clean, washed. White is the color of the robes given to the saints at rest. Standard conservative interpretation sees this as either the

antichrist himself or the government which will be used by the antichrist when the antichrist fully reveals himself. Either way this is the beast. However, the people on earth without heaven's perspective probably will not realize it. The traditional conservative, protestant, dispensational, fundamentalist interpretation, which I follow, is that the bow without arrows means that the beast uses the threat of military force without actually using military force. The crown is the normal word for crown, a victor's crown. It is for the winner of a contest or battle and is like the crowns we will receive at the judgment seat of Christ. It is not a diadem, a royal crown.

So the rider of the white horse bent on conquest was successful in conquering much of the earth. This is the period spoken of by Daniel, the signing of the covenant with Israel to reinstitute temple sacrifices for one week (Daniel 9:27), which is seven years. This ruler which shall come is, like the rider on the white horse, either the antichrist himself or the government which will be controlled by the antichrist (the beast) after he reveals himself. This covenant ushers in a period of peace, which lasts for about three and one half years (Daniel 9:27). At that time the Antichrist will break the covenant and no longer permit sacrifices.

3-4) This ushers in the period of the red horse. The living creature issuing this command is the second living creature, which has the face of an ox. Since I do not believe that anyone on earth will be aware of the actual opening of the seals, the command to John to, "Come," is for the believers in heaven to observe the events on earth. Neither do I believe that anyone on earth with see a physical, material fiery red horse. The rider on the fiery red horse was given power to take peace from the earth. We do not know when this rider goes forth, but in Daniel 9:27 we are told that in the middle of the week the antichrist will put an end to sacrifices and set up the abomination which causes desolation, which ends the covenant that began the seventieth week. Most commentators believe that this fiery red horse is the middle of the week recorded by Daniel. This assumes that the end of sacrifices causes the end of the Antichrist's peace. I personally believe that this taking of peace from the earth is the breakdown of governmental authority: anarchy, not war. I believe that this will be going on throughout the first part of the tribulation. Perhaps the rising anarchy will even be the cause of the Antichrist breaking the covenant. That I do not know, but I am certain that the rider's large sword, which symbolizes men slaying each other, is crime, riots and other results of anarchy, not war, and begins much earlier than the middle of the tribulation. The sword throughout the Scriptures represents men killing other men. In Romans 13, the sword represents human government's responsibility to execute convicted criminals even though Rome executed very few criminals with a sword. The statement that the rider's sword is large means that this violence will be on a large scale.

So the beast deceives his way into power by offering peace, but the results of his policies are just the opposite.

This, I believe, begins the period of time called, in Chapter Seven, the great tribulation.

5-6) The first living creature was like a lion, the second like an ox and the third had the face of a man. While the living creatures (beasts KJV) like a lion, ox and eagle each had the appearance of a lion, ox and eagle respectively, with six wings and covered with eyes, this third living creature is said to have the face of a man (4:7). This implies that he has the body of some kind of beast and not the body of a man. This third living creature now tells John to, "Come."

When the Lamb opens the third seal, John sees a black horse. Black is first mentioned in Genesis 1:2, where the word darkness can be translated black. The scales represent commerce, but not just any commerce. Everywhere else in the Word of God this word translated scales, is translated yoke. The entire economy of the world is yoked together, even today. This is a breakdown in the ability be yoked together, probably because of the anarchy of the second seal. Because of the breakdown in the money supply, transportation, trust, etc., material want will come to the earth and the basic necessities, represented by the wheat (middle class) and the barley (the food of the poor), will become very expensive. However, the oil and the wine, representing the rich, will not be touched.

Also, the wording implies that there will a problem with obtaining the wheat and the barley, but the supply of wheat and barley will not be diminished.

7-8) When the lamb opens the fourth seal, the fourth and last living creature commands John to, “Come!” This horse is pale and the rider was named Death, and Hades was following close behind him. A few people died under each of the first three horses. This rider, however, killed one fourth of the earth. They were killed by sword, famine and plague, and by the wild beasts of the earth. There will not be any more wild beasts than there are now. There might even be fewer. The anarchy caused by the second seal and the breakdown in commerce causing material want causes more anarchy and organized raids, which cause famine and plague. People will be unable to defend themselves against wild beasts and the wild beasts will be driven by hunger and the great number of human carcasses to attack people. There is nothing to indicate that this will either be concentrated in certain geographic areas or spread throughout the world.

9-11) When the lamb opened the fifth seal, no living creature commanded, “Come!” Instead of going somewhere to see something, John saw immediately before him the souls of those slain because of the word of God. Since the dead in Christ were raised at the rapture, these martyrs became believers since then, probably three to three and one half years. These will not be ‘silent witnesses,’ but are slain because of ... the testimony they had maintained. At this point they are told to wait because others will join them. Under the altar alludes to the animals slain on the altar as a sacrifice to God. Since a white robe is the righteousness of Christ, which they are given at this time, I do not know why they must wait to join the fellowship of all believers. Nor do I know where under the altar is.

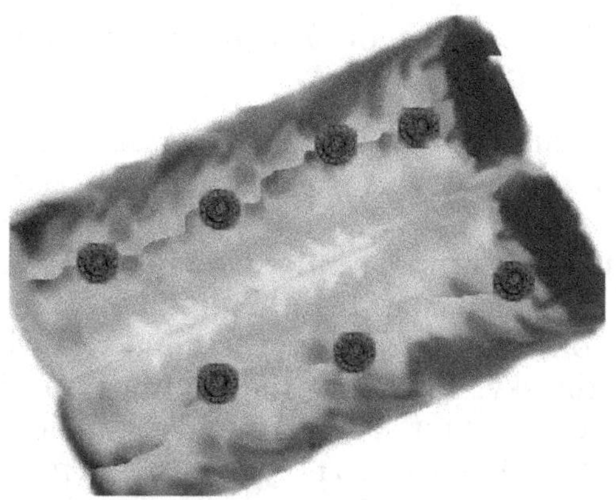

Though we are not to take vengeance, the Lord will take vengeance for us. The question these martyrs ask is simply, “How long?” The answer was equally simple: “Until their number ... was completed.” There will be martyrs until Jesus Christ returns to earth and His feet touch the Mount of Olives (Zechariah 14:4). This will be the end of what we call the battle of Armageddon, when Satan will be bound in the Abyss for one thousand years. This will be the beginning of the Millennium.

12-14) I watched as he opened the sixth seal. This is the first seal of which the Scriptures say that John watched its opening. From the point of view of the unregenerate on earth, this will probably be the first seal that will have immediate results. This is the last seal with direct results.

The seventh seal, opened in 8:1, has no direct results; it is the beginning of the seven trumpet judgments.

Perhaps for the first time in history, one earthquake will be felt all over the earth. The sun becomes dark and the moon becomes blood red. There is almost endless speculation as to what causes this. Though we know that God is the primary cause, we have no information in the Word of God as to the means God uses to cause the earthquake, the blackened sun and the blood red moon.

Most commentators believe that the stars falling are meteors even though this is usual word for star. They point out the word meteor or meteorite is not in the Greek NT.

A more difficult concept is the sky receding like a scroll. The NASB translates this word 'split apart'. The only other place it occurs in the New Testament is Acts 15:39 where Paul and Barnabas parted company. Paul and Barnabas had been close together and now they could no longer see one another. This is the same idea with the earth and the sky. Somehow, the relationship with the atmosphere and outer space will make stars and clouds seem much further away. The phrase every mountain and island was removed from its place emphasizes that the earthquake is over the entire earth and that all of these judgments are related, taking place at the same time.

15-17) I do not believe that those remaining on earth will use these exact words. They will remain in unbelief and will firmly believe that the one causing these judgments will be their enemy. They will hide from Him and be afraid of Him, but will not view Him as the lamb slain from the foundation of the world. They will view the Lamb as the enemy of all mankind.

Chapter Seven

All of Chapter Seven is an answer the question at the end of Chapter Six: who can stand?

1) Please do not assume that the four corners of the earth are geographic locations. This phrase occurs several times in the Word of God and each time it means the whole earth or the entire earth. So the four corners are probably North, South, East and West. This is the normal word for angel, and they are said to have the power to harm the earth (v 3). This is also the normal word for a very strong wind, a storm. So the standard interpretation is that these angels release the storm of the wrath of God. The remaining judgments will hit the earth with the speed and force of a storm. Since these are the judgments of God, the angels simply release these winds at the proper time. They do not create the judgments. This does not mean that there is no wind at all anywhere on earth at this time, but that the judgments of God are held back.

2) The next angel comes from the east and calls out with a great (loud) voice. Once again this cry makes those who can hear it responsible for what they hear. An east wind, that is a wind coming out of the east, throughout Scriptures is a judgment of God. Jesus Christ will return to the Mount of Olives east of Jerusalem (Zechariah 14:4) and it will split from east to west. The magi came from the east (Matthew 2:1). Job was the greatest of the men of the East, the door of the tabernacle and the door of the temple both faced east.

As for the seal of the living God, we do not know what it will look like. The seal itself will, however, be something visible to people on earth. Perhaps people will even be able to see the angels.

3) God's judgments are restrained until the servants of our God are sealed. The seal on the forehead will be clearly visible to others. The judgments on the land, sea and trees will destroy the earth's environment because of mankind's sin. When the sealing is complete, the judgments will begin.

4-8) Those who were sealed: 144,000 from all the tribes of Israel. It is unfortunate that most people who comment on this passage 'spiritualize' this section. What is written is simple and clear. The Word of God says what it means and means what it says. This is the beginning of the fulfillment of all the prophecies to the nation of Israel.

There is no reason given for the selection of these particular twelve tribes. Jacob, Israel, had twelve sons; Reuben, Simeon, Gad, Judah, Issachar, Zebulun, Levi, Dan, Asher, Naphtali, Joseph and Benjamin. Joseph was given the right of the firstborn, a double portion. Joseph's two sons, Ephraim and Manasseh, each had a portion as a full tribe. Each complete listing of the twelve tribes in the Scriptures always lists twelve tribes, no more or less. However, the lists include many different combinations. Usually Levi is omitted. Here in Revelation 7 Dan is omitted.

This sealing of the 144,000 means that the beast cannot harm them. They will live through the judgments of God, at least the first ones.

9-17) After this I looked. After the rapture of the Church, after the beast comes to power, after the first six seals are opened, after the 144,000 Israelites are sealed, John sees a great multitude in heaven. Since Chapter Seven answers the question at the end of Chapter Six, who can stand? This great multitude stood for the Lamb during the tribulation and gave their lives.

Verse fourteen is only time the phrase great tribulation occurs in the Word of God. The great tribulation begins when the Antichrist, the beast, cuts off the sacrifices in the temple in the middle of the seven year period we call the tribulation or the seventieth week of Daniel. Remember, the tribulation or the seventieth week of Daniel begins with the signing of a covenant, a treaty, which allows the restarting of temple sacrifices by the Jews in Jerusalem.

The promise that they will never thirst, hunger or experience scorching heat ever again probably tells how they were martyred. The only question is, are these the souls under the altar (6:9) or is this after there number is complete? I believe that this scene in heaven is after their number is complete. I believe that when the seventh seal is opened, the remaining judgments will take place very rapidly.

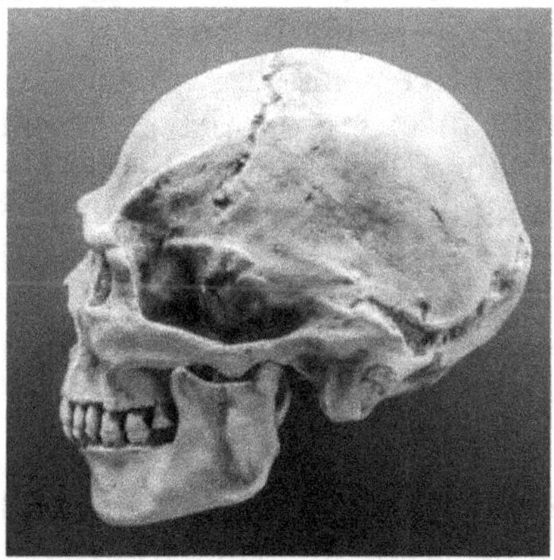

Chapter Eight

1) The only immediate result of the opening of the seventh seal was silence in heaven for about half an hour. I believe that the trumpet and bowl judgments take place very rapidly, perhaps concluding in a few days. This silence is heaven preparing for the final judgments. There is no indication that this half an hour has any kind of symbolical or 'heavenly' meaning. I believe that this very brief time of preparation divides the activity of heaven between the preparation of the saints in heaven and the preparation of the earth for the saints.

2) Instead of an immediate judgment, seven angels prepare another series of judgments, the seven trumpet judgments. The angels did not have the power to judge themselves; the trumpets were given to them. Before there was television, radio, printed books and newspapers or even public address systems, there were

trumpets. The blast of a trumpet could mean the arrival of a king. It could be the beginning of a festival. Or it could mean danger. Trumpets were the signals of important events until around one hundred years ago.

3-5) Before the seven angels do anything with the trumpets, another angel comes to the altar. This is not the brazen altar of the courtyard of both the tabernacle and the temple where the blood of animal sacrifices was poured out and their bodies burned. This is the golden altar of the Holy Place where only incense was burned. The smoke of the incense from the golden altar was necessary to fill the Holy of Holies before the High Priest could enter it on his annual visit. Aaron once used a censer to fill the Holy of Holies with smoke, like the censer used by this angel (Leviticus 16). The incense this angel is offering is different from just the prayers of the saints because the prayers are mingled together with the incense.

Are these the prayers of all the saints throughout all time, the prayers of only the tribulation saints, the prayers of the saints alive on earth at that time or only those prayers being prayed at that time? This seems to be prayers for salvation and vengeance since God claims vengeance as His right, not the right of the saints. I believe that the peals of thunder, rumblings, flashes of lightning and an earthquake take place on earth, the inhabitants of the earth see them and that these happen after the judgments of the six seals.

6) The seven angels with the trumpets had to wait for the angel with the censer before they even prepare to sound their trumpets. As each trumpet is sounded, the judgment will be immediate and visible to the inhabitants of the earth.

7) The first angel sounded his trumpet. The preparation and warnings are over: silence in heaven for half an hour, the angel hurling the golden censer to earth and the seven angels preparing to sound. Even the seal judgments are not direct judgments from God. What most people regard as the great tribulation begins with this trumpet.

The plagues of Egypt are only a type of these judgments on the entire earth. The plague of hail on Egypt had thunder and lightning on the land of Egypt only. With this trumpet judgment, there is hail throughout the world. If the fire of this plague is not lightning, then it is much more than lightning and it is mixed with blood.

Peter quotes Joel in his sermon at Pentecost and says about this time signs ... blood and the moon shall be turned to blood. (Acts 2:19, 20) These are the only New Testament references outside of Revelation where the word blood refers to something other than a man or animal with its blood. Concerning these references to the moon turning to blood, raining blood, water turning to blood, etc. there are only two explanations. The first is that the plague on Egypt of the water turning to blood is just a type of what will come during the great tribulation and that all of these references to blood will be miraculously, literally fulfilled with blood, as the first plague on Egypt was fulfilled. The second explanation is that the word blood in these passages is used like it is in Genesis 49:11 where Judah is prophesied to wash his robes in the blood of grapes. Blood would be symbolical of the life juices of whatever was referenced; i.e. the blood of the moon might be lava or dust in the earth's atmosphere which colors the moon blood red. Most commentators believe that this word blood is symbolical. I believe that this is a miracle of literal blood.

There is no reason to assume that a third of the earth, trees and all (all does not have to mean one hundred percent, it can mean only most or majority) the green grass being burned up is anything other than what the word of God says. This 'destruction of the environment' is a direct judgment of God on the earth for man's sin and rebellion against Him. Also, there is nothing to indicate that this judgment has any relation to any other judgment. It is possible that this fire and hail is part of some physical phenomena which causes some of the later plagues, but perhaps this plague is different from all the others.

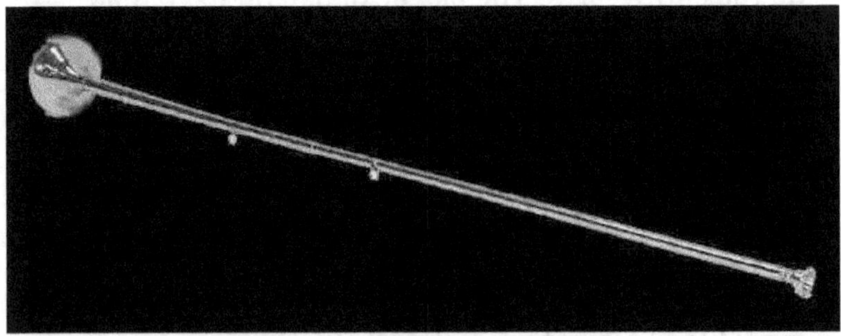

8-9) When the second angel makes a loud trumpet blast to announce his judgment, a great flaming meteorite or comet hits the ocean. Though it does tremendous damage, it does not end life on earth. In fact, only a third of the ships in the sea and a third of marine life died. The true miracle is that the destruction is no greater than it is. Once again, there are two possibilities for this blood. The blood is either the 'blood of the earth,' red lava or a supernatural event which changes the water into blood. Though it could be the blood of the sea creatures mixed with something else (perhaps a red tide?), this would be as miraculous as changing the water into actual blood.

10-11) When the third angel sounds his loud trumpet blast, a great star falls from heaven and pollutes a third of the potable water supply. So what is different about this great star and the flaming mountain of the second trumpet? In verse eight the word, though sometimes translated hill, is the normal word for mountain. The same word for blaze is used in verses eight and ten, though it modifies the word fire in verse eight and lamp in verse ten. The emphasis in the second trumpet judgment is on the heat of the fire, while the emphasis in the third trumpet judgment is on the light. They could both be meteorites, the second judgment larger and slower, since the Greek language calls any heavenly object a star, other than the sun or the moon.

When the waters turn bitter, it means that they are poisoned, not just bad tasting. The name for this star, Wormwood, is frequently used in literature to name someone who poisons the mind of someone else.

This star poisons a third of all the fresh water on earth; the previous star fell on sea.

12) When the fourth angel sounded his trumpet a judgment similar to the opening of the sixth seal falls on the earth. Many use this as an excuse to deny the literal interpretation of the entire book of Revelation. They argue that if the sun was already black like sackcloth

made of hair then how could a third of the sun turn dark at this time?

I see two possible answers. The first is that the sun did not stay black like sackcloth but returned to luminance sometime before this fourth trumpet judgment. There is nothing in the Word of God to support this except that John obviously saw events on earth after the during and after the opening of the sixth seal. Also, there is nothing in the Word of God to indicate how long from the opening of the sixth seal until the sounding of the fourth trumpet. The second possible answer is that we do not interpret black like sackcloth made of goat hair properly. Instead of a complete absence of light, the proper interpretation would be something like twilight or immediate predawn, perhaps even brighter. Perhaps both interpretations are partially correct. However, the word translated black in Chapter Six is only found six places in the New Testament and is usually translated 'ink.'

According to the Scriptures, at the sounding of the fourth trumpet, the sun is visible, at least partially. The third of the sun, moon and stars darkening can mean that the third approximately one third of the physical light is obscured from the sun, the moon and the stars. It might mean that all of the stars, the sun and moon are still visible but their overall light is reduced by one third or it might mean that they all appear to shrink in size. I believe, however, that end of the verse explains the rest of the verse. A third part of the day and a third part of the night will be darkness, otherwise the sun, moon and stars will not change at this judgment.

13) The flying eagle pronouncing the three woes is, like the prophets of Israel, pronouncing the judgments of God on the earth. Letting the inhabitants of earth know about these coming judgments is another opportunity to repent. It is also alerting the inhabitants of the earth of the increase in severity of the judgments. All of the judgments on ancient Israel are but types, shadows of the judgments to come.

Part Five: Chapters Nine and Ten

Chapter Nine

1-2) The fifth angel sounded his trumpet. Verse twelve tells us that this fifth trumpet is the first woe of the three woes proclaimed by the eagle flying in midair. The sixth trumpet is the second woe and the seventh trumpet is the third woe. A "woe" in the Word of God means a judgment of God. It is always a judgment for unrepentant sin; usually the final judgment for those hardened in unbelief after repeated opportunities to repent.

The words for star, fallen, sky and earth are all common, general words. There is nothing unusual about these words. The problem for us today is that although each of these words can mean many things, none of these meanings are out of the ordinary. For example, the word translated sky is usually translated heaven, but can also be translated air.

This has given rise to many different conclusions as commentators for nearly two thousand years have examined the various aspects of Revelation chapter nine. Rather than looking at any interpretation or speculating about the unclear, a few things are obvious. This star is a being, not an astronomical object. This being opposes God. This being was in heaven then fell to earth. This happens at the sounding of the fifth trumpet; it is not historical from our perspective so it cannot refer to Satan and the garden of Eden. It might refer to the war in Heaven when Michael the Archangel casts Satan out of Heaven (Revelation 12).

At this time the star is given something or some power which allowed beings from some part of the underworld (shaft or well of the Abyss) to come to the earth. This power (key) was not taken by force, but the power (key) was given to it at this time late in the great tribulation. Physical, material smoke rose from the Abyss because the smoke darkens the sun and the sky. Once again, we do not know if the sun had recovered from the earlier plagues of darkness or if this is in addition to them. This word for Abyss always refers to the same thing. The English word Hell, the Hebrew word Sheol and the Greek word Hades all refer to the unseen spiritual world. Part of that world is the place of departed spirits.

Those who died in Christ are in blessing and those who died without Christ are even now in a place of torment. There is, however, much more to this unseen world. This part of Hell called the Abyss seems to be the dwelling place of some of the worst beings of Hell. While they are truly demonic, they are not the demons which are free to roam the earth today. These creatures of the Abyss are locked in there for now and will stay in the Abyss until this star opens the Abyss with a key at the sounding of the fifth trumpet judgment.

The word open is the usual word for open. Beings that had been locked in the Abyss are now free to roam the earth. People on earth will see them as material beings, not ghosts or spirits. Some commentators believe that there is such a tremendous number of these beings that what appears to John as smoke is nothings more than this cloud of locusts. Whatever this smoke is, it will be visible to people on earth and this smoke darkens the sun and sky.

3) The only other time in the Word of God this word locusts appears is the food of John the Baptist. Nothing about these creatures, as they are described, resembles a locust except that they swarm. Proverbs 30:27 tells us that locusts have no king, yet they advance together in ranks. These locusts, however, are led by a king.

We are not told how large these locusts are but verse seven says that they looked like horses. Since these creatures of the Abyss are called locusts, we must assume that in every way they are not described they look and act like locusts. They would be the size of locusts, would fly like locusts and would swarm like locusts.

I believe that these creatures had power for five months (verses 5 & 10) because they will be released from the Abyss only five months before the end of the tribulation. They have power until Jesus Christ returns to earth. Those who believe that the five-month reign of these locusts begins earlier in the great tribulation have no information in the Word of God as to what stops them.

The locusts came down upon the earth from out of the smoke. They rise out of the Abyss in smoke, cover the entire earth darkening the sun and sky, then drop down from the sky onto the earth with power like that of scorpions of the earth. This is the normal, usual word for scorpions. The word power, however, is usually translated authority or right, as when Christ says All authority is given unto me. What is the authority or right of a scorpion? God has given a scorpion the right, authority, power to inject poison into its prey.

Cylinder Seal with Scorpion Man Shooting at Winged Creatures
Walters Art Museum Public Domain

4) So the people who did not have the seal of God on their foreheads are the legitimate prey of these locusts. Unlike locusts, which feed upon plants, these creatures could not harm the grass of the earth or any plant or tree. Though fish and animals are not mentioned, we can

assume that the scorpions cannot harm them either, since they are not the natural prey of scorpions. They might not be completely exempt, since present-day scorpions can sting animals.

5-6) These locusts have the specific authority, power, right to torture people who did not have the seal of God on their foreheads but not to kill them. While this seems like horrible cruelty to us, God is giving these people another chance to repent. Instead of repenting, most people attempt suicide but are unable to die. This only lasts five months, but this will be five months of intense pain. As long as they are still alive, they have the opportunity to repent. Death will return with the sixth trumpet judgment and the seven bowl judgments just a few days before Christ returns.

7-10) The best interpretation is no interpretation. Take these words to mean what they say. These creatures are repeatedly called locusts, so there is no reason to believe that they are anything other than locusts. They have, however, some very unusual features. They are adorned for battle like a horse would be. The text does not say that they have four legs, a neck, a mane, and a body like a horse even though they might. All that it says it that they are adorned for battle like a horse would be. In the same way, the text does not say that they had crowns of gold, but something like crowns of gold. This might mean that they wore something like crowns of gold or it might mean that part of their anatomy looked something like crowns of gold. Their faces resembled human faces with hair like women's hair. That would be long flowing hair. Though they have teeth like lion's teeth, there is no indication that they use these teeth on men. Perhaps they do; the text does not say. They also wear breastplates like breastplates of iron. Like the crowns of gold, the text does not say that the breastplates are iron breastplates, but like breastplates of iron. Like the crowns of gold, this could be part of their anatomy. Also, the sound of their wings was like the thundering of many horses and chariots rushing into battle. With the tremendous number of these creatures, this sound can probably be heard everywhere on earth. As the tail is described, stings like scorpions, once again their time is limited to five months. Most stinging or biting insects sting either with their mouths, such as a horsefly, or with their tails aiming downward, such as a wasp. Only a scorpion stings with its tail coming over the top and forward.

No reason is given as to why the star wants to open the abyss or why the locusts want to torment men or what they hope to accomplish under their king, except that at this time Satan knows that his time is short.

11) The Greek Apollyon (Apollyon--Destroyer), the name for the angel of the Abyss, the king of the locusts, is not found anywhere else in the Word of God. However the Hebrew Abaddon (Abbadon--Destruction) appears several times in the Old Testament. Every time it is translated Destruction.

The traditional interpretation of those who believe that the book of Revelation should be interpreted literally is that the star falling from heaven with the key to the Abyss is Satan himself. Revelation twelve, where Satan is at war with Michael and is cast out of heaven, is just another view of the same event. After using his key to release the locusts from the Abyss, Satan himself becomes their king. I see no reason for not accepting the traditional point of view. If we hold that the king of the Abyss is not Satan, but an angel under Satan, what difference does that make?

The important point is that these creatures do not act randomly. They have a king and a purpose.

12) These judgments are called woes. They are more severe than anything up to this point. These are like the plagues on Egypt under Moses where in the beginning Pharaoh hardened his own heart before God hardened Pharaoh's heart. While the early judgments were in a

sense the natural consequences of certain sins, God is directly bringing these judgments. For example, when men accepted the leadership of the rider on the white (first) horse, the next three horses inevitably follow. Now mankind's heart is hardened and all mankind face two more woes.

13) The second woe is the sixth angel sounding his trumpet. As the trumpet sounded, John heard a voice coming from the horns of the golden altar that is before God. Animal sacrifices were offered on the brazen altar, the altar of bronze in the courtyard. This, however, is the golden altar in the holy place just outside of the curtain which separated it from the holy of holies. The golden altar was usually called the altar of incense because the smoke which obscured the ark of the covenant came from it. It is much smaller than the brazen altar, only one cubit long by one cubit wide and two cubits tall. It was made of acacia wood and overlaid with gold. Incense is the prayers of the saints in Revelation 5:8.

The emphasis here is on the gold (royalty, deity) and on the horns of the altar. Horns are the strength and power of the animal. So the voice coming from the horn of the golden altar is a prayer to God, speaking with royal, divine power.

It knows that what it asks will happen, so it speaks with confident authority.

14) The angel who sounded the sixth trumpet was commanded to release four wicked angels bound at the great river Euphrates. None of the previous five angels who sounded trumpets had any responsibilities after they sounded their trumpets. What does release mean and how could a holy angel do it? Is there any significance to four angels? What is meant by bound at the great river Euphrates?

Every first year student of Greek is taught 'never base your theology on a preposition.' The word *epi,* occurs seven hundred eighty times in the New Testament and is translated by dozens of English words such as on, at, to, over, for, against, of, before, upon and by. So the four angels are bound on or at or to or over or for or against or before or upon or by the great river Euphrates. Also, the word *deo,* translated here as bound is translated in other places tied, prisoners, ties up, arrest, chained, married.

I can see only one way a river, any river, can bind an angel. As we learn throughout the Word of God, but especially in Daniel, every empire of man is controlled by a spiritual being. If a nation yields itself to the Spirit of God, then God's Holy Spirit will direct it. If a ruler is deluded into thinking that he rules in his own might, then he is controlled by a demon. I believe that these four angels are the spiritual forces and that the binding of the great river Euphrates is the river flowing and preventing armies from crossing it. So the releasing of the four angels is the drying up of the river to allow the armies of verse sixteen to cross.

It also means that the it is time for these evil angels to go throughout the earth with their demonic mounted troops to force men to the battle on the great day of God Almighty.

The number four might refer to four nations, the four winds of heaven, meaning the entire earth, or it might simply be four wicked angels with no significance to the number beyond that.

It is not reasonable to believe that the Euphrates is dried up twice. Revelation sixteen, however, describes the sixth angel pouring out the sixth bowl judgment and drying up the Euphrates River to prepare the way for the kings of the East as part of the preparation for the battle on the great day of God Almighty. Explaining this apparent contradiction requires understanding two often overlooked facts. The seventh trumpet judgment, which is the next trumpet judgment, is all seven of the bowl judgments. These bowl judgments all take place very rapidly; probably in a matter of days. So the first fact is that the sixth trumpet judgment described here is less than two weeks from the sixth bowl judgment, probably much less. From the standpoint of people on earth, these two separate judgments will look like the same judgment. The second often overlooked fact is that the sixth bowl judgment mentions just three powerful demons who influence human beings while the beings described here at the sixth trumpet judgment are not human beings. The demons and angels of hell must be released before the humans gather for the battle on the great day of God Almighty. We only see the material world. We do not see the very real spiritual forces which cause great changes in the material world.

15) This hour and day and month and year are during the five months that the locusts which sting like scorpions are tormenting the earth. Those who believe that the first woe ends before this woe begins point to the statement that during the first woe men will seek death but be unable to find it while under this woe a third of mankind will be killed. I believe that they are simply allowing too

much time for this sixth trumpet judgment. Though death returns while the locusts are still on the earth it is only for a few hours or at the most a few days.

16) These two hundred million mounted troops could be the number of the demonic horsemen or they could be the humans gathered at the sixth bowl judgment. The creatures which are described in verses seventeen and following are certainly not human and they are the creatures which are led by the four angels to kill one third of mankind. Beyond any question, comparing this sixth trumpet judgment with the sixth bowl judgment, there are first demonic horsemen followed by human armies. There is no reason in the text to interpret any of these creatures as symbolic of modern human warfare.

The number was given to John so that he could record it with certainty. There was no possible way for him to count or even estimate that many mounted troops.

17-19) Contrasting the demonic locusts, these demonic horsemen had the power to kill one third of everyone still alive at this point.

The words for the colors of their breastplates do not occur anywhere else in the Scriptures, so we cannot know for certain what each color symbolizes, if anything. Like the locusts, the best interpretation is no interpretation. These are demonic creatures and John is describing them to the best of his ability. These horses and riders had breastplates, probably one for each rider and one for each horse. The heads of the horses resembled the heads of lions, and out of their mouths came fire, smoke and sulfur. Also, their tails were like snakes, having heads with which they inflict injury. They killed and injured people with their heads and tails.

The Scriptures are not clear as to whether the people on earth see these demons as demons, or if they will only see the human soldiers of the sixth bowl judgment. I believe that the timing of the seven bowl judgments is very rapid. So even though the release of the demonic spirits bound by the Euphrates and the human armies are different, there will be very little time between them. From only a few days to at most a few weeks, people on earth will probably see the time between the release of the demonic horsemen and the human soldiers so short that they will view them as one event.

This entire book is called the Revelation. It reveals the way things really are, not what humanity sees. These demonic horsemen, whether visible to unregenerate humanity or not, actually kill one third of mankind. These demonic horsemen also inflict painful injuries on others who are not killed.

20) Rudolph Boultman called the God of the Old Testament, Jehovah, YHWH, a bloody bully. For those like Boultman who refuse to reconcile the seemingly opposite truths that God is a God of love as well as a just and holy God who cannot dwell in the presence of sin this verse explains why each of these judgments must come. The rest of mankind ... still did not repent of the work of their hands. God is not wanting anyone to perish, but everyone to come to repentance. (2 Peter 3:9) Everyone who refuses to repent will face the judgment of God. These judgments are not some form of sadistic pleasure where God delights in torturing people, as Satan

would have us believe. These judgments are a necessary result of the rebellion of hardened hearts.

Since the 1960s, the Western cultures have seen a tremendous growth in direct demon worship. From Satanism to New Age, it is more open every year. Idolatry is putting anything before God and even when we do not realize what we are doing, idolatry is demon worship.

21) This list of sins which bring on the remaining judgments are murder, magic arts *pharmakon*, which can also mean the use of drugs or poisons, sexual immorality *porneia,* the general term for fornication from which we get the word pornography, or their thefts.

Chapter Ten

1) This angel's appearance to John begins a series of visions interrupting the narrative of the plagues, which resumes in chapter 15. For now, John sees events which will not be visible to the unregenerate on earth during the great tribulation.

John sees a great, strong, mighty angel descending to earth. Everything is for John; there is no record that anyone else sees this angel. This angel is not identified for us.

The angel's clothing is a cloud. Clouds veil heaven from earth and much about this angel is hidden from us. Clouds also symbolize the divide, the doorway, between heaven and earth. Elijah went up to heaven in a whirlwind, Ezekiel saw God above the clouds, the mount of transfiguration was in a cloud, the Lord went up to heaven in a cloud, the angels returned to announce his departure in a cloud and the Lord will return to earth two times in clouds; once for His saints (the rapture) and once to set up His kingdom.

He has a rainbow above his head. The rainbow is God's symbol of His covenant with all mankind not to destroy the earth again with water. It encircles God's throne in heaven, both in Revelation and in Ezekiel's vision. His face like the sun and legs like pillars of fire are similar to John's vision of Jesus Christ in Chapter One. The similarity is so strong, that many believe that this is another vision of Christ. Except for this description of the angel's appearance, there is no other reason to believe that he is Christ. When he speaks (v 6), he sounds like a created being, not God Himself.

Everything about this mighty angel shines with the glory of heaven. But the glory of heaven is also the holiness of heaven, which cannot dwell in the presence of sin.

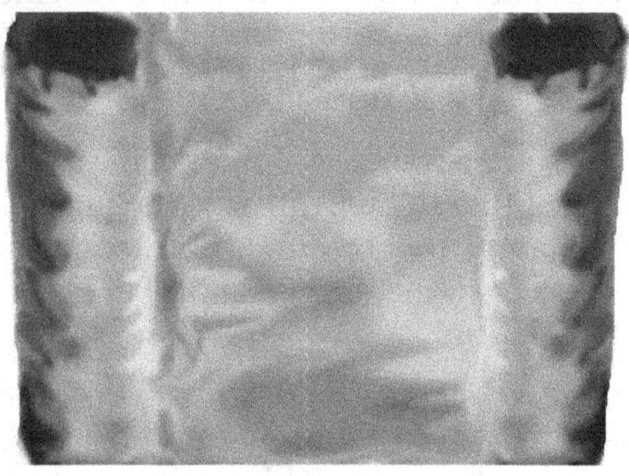

2) There has been much speculation about what this little scroll is which the angel holds in his hand. It is called a little scroll, though in verse 8 the voice from heaven simply calls it a scroll. Based on Jeremiah 15:16 When your words came, I ate them, this little scroll contains words of God, but probably not what we have as the Word of God. The speculation of Seiss that this is the instructions to the angel are as good a guess as anything, but fail to explain why they tasted sweet in John's mouth but made his stomach sour. We must admit that we cannot be certain what is written on the scroll.

It lay open, so whatever its message, during the great tribulation it will be exposed.

The angel placed, put, planted his right foot on the sea and his left foot on the land. Throughout most of the

Word of God the sea and the land mean the material sea and land made of water and earth. In the book of Revelation, however, the word sea or waters sometimes means the raging sea of ungoverned humanity (17:15, 13:1). When the word sea is used this way with the word land, the word land means the stable, orderly control of government. This is probably a double meaning here. With his feet planted on the material, physical sea and land he is standing in control of God's creation. With his feet planted on the raging sea of humanity and the governments of this world, he has authority over all mankind.

3) The shout of the angel was like the roar of a lion. The deep base roar of a lion can be heard over a mile away. Everyone near will notice this shout, which causes the seven thunders to speak.

4) Forbidding John to write down what the seven thunders spoke reminds us that even with this Revelation, we still do not know about most of what goes on during the great tribulation. Not only the seven thunders, but most of the details of everything else are hidden.

5-6) By lifting his right hand to heaven, the angel is making the most solemn oath possible. The description of Jesus Christ is an expansion of the formula found throughout the book of Revelation: Who is, lives for ever and ever; who was, who created the heavens ... the earth ... and the sea and all that is in it; and who is to come, There will be no more delay.

7) If there was any doubt that this is the fulfillment of the prophecies of the Old Testament, this assures us that it is.

8-10) The voice which John had heard from heaven commanding him not write down what the seven thunders spoke now commanded him to take the little scroll and eat it. Eating this book symbolizes taking the contents of the book and letting it become a part of John. The most reasonable explanation seems to me that the little scroll is this vision of Jesus Christ which we call the book of Revelation up to this point. It is a comfort to John as he is given the vision, as sweet as honey in John's mouth. But the realization of the judgment of God on unbelievers and all creation makes it turn John's stomach sour.

11) This command/promise to John that he would still prophecy, the book of Revelation is almost half finished, makes me believe that the little scroll is only what John had written up to this point. It also shows that John had a rest from his vision; that the next part beginning with Chapter 11 is given to John sometime later.

Part Six: Chapters Eleven and Twelve

Part Six: Chapters Eleven and Twelve

Chapter Eleven

1) John represents the Church throughout the book of Revelation. As he represents all believers in Chapter Ten when he eats the little scroll, so he represents all believers when he takes the reed like a measuring rod. Ezekiel, in a vision, saw a man with a linen cord and a measuring rod measure the millennial temple (Ez. 40:3). Later, John sees an angel with a measuring rod of gold measure the New Jerusalem (Rev. 21:15). But this is the temple of the Great Tribulation, where the abomination that causes desolation is set up. This is probably after the temple has been cleansed from the abomination but before the Lord returns.

We are never told how many worshipers are in the temple area, but there are so few worshipers that they can be counted. This is just before the seventh trumpet judgment, which includes all seven bowl judgments. This seems to be the beginning of the 45-day period Daniel records at the close of his book (Daniel 12:11,12).

The tribulation begins with the signing of the covenant (Daniel 9:27) which re-institutes the daily sacrifices. There is some disagreement as to whether this refers to the signing of the covenant or the actual beginning of the sacrifices. Probably there will be so little time between the two events that no one will notice a time gap.

2) The outer court that John was commanded to exclude refers to the time period of the abomination that causes desolation. The Gentiles will trample the holy city for forty-two months. This time is given in months, not weeks or days, because this is not as precise. It will probably begin on a certain day in the middle of the 70th week of Daniel when the sacrifices will be cut off. But the end of this period of the gentiles will be a series of events culminating in the return of Jesus Christ to the earth when his feet touch the mount of olives and the mountain splits in two from the east to the west (Zech. 14:4).

3) Who are the two witnesses and when do they minister? Though the Scriptures do not tell us who these men are, they minister during the tribulation. They are mature believers who were not caught up at the Rapture. All believers are caught up ... to meet the Lord in the air (I Thess. 4:17). The Greek word harpazo, translated into English as caught up is rapturo in Latin, from which we get the English word Rapture. In I Cor. 15:51 Paul says we shall not all sleep, but we shall all be changed–in a flash, in the twinkling of an eye, at the last trumpet.

Since the Word of God clearly states that these two witnesses are not left behind during the Rapture, this is a problem for many. Some, such as Tim LaHaye, ignore I Cor. 15 and I Thess. 4 and say that these men begin their ministry before the Rapture and signing of the covenant with reinstitution of daily sacrifices in Jerusalem. This means that they end their ministry in the middle of the Tribulation, around the time of the abomination that causes desolation and the ending of sacrifices and offerings. Revelation 11:3 begins with the word *and,* tying the 42 months of the Gentiles (the second half of the tribulation) to the ministry of the two witnesses. Also, Revelation 11:14 states that the conclusion of their ministry is the end of the second woe, sixth trumpet judgment, and the beginning of the third woe which is the seventh trumpet judgment which is all seven of the bowl judgments. I believe that the beginning of their ministries will be tied to the cutting off of the daily sacrifices and the setting up of the abomination that causes desolation.

Others hold that these two witnesses were unbelievers at the time of the rapture who were converted soon after. They would have a strong background in the Word of God but no saving faith until after the rapture. They might grow up in godly homes and still be quite young at the time of the rapture. Daniel, with his three friends, was probably only 15 or 16 when he was taken to Babylon and stood before Nebuchadnezzar.

Most conservatives however believe that these two witnesses are resurrected prophets. Hebrews 9:27 says that man is destined to die once and so some believe that these two are Enoch and Elijah, since neither of these men tasted death. Others point to Moses and Elijah with Jesus on the Mount of Transfiguration (Matthew 17:3) and say that the type of miracles performed by the two men means that they must be Moses and Elijah. Moses struck Egypt, the type of this world, with ten plagues, including turning the water into blood. Elijah called down the fire of God from heaven at the battle against

Baal worship on Mount Carmel and on the two Captains and companies of fifty men. He also prayed and the Lord shut up the sky, causing a drought in Israel.

The absolute, authoritative Word of God does not identify these two witnesses. In the middle of the tribulation they reveal themselves by their signs. They wear sackcloth, burlap bags, to show disregard for materialism while dressing modestly.

4) Zechariah saw two olive trees on the right and left of a lampstand (Zech. 4:2,3). He asked an angel twice what they were (4:11,12) and was told These are the two who are anointed to serve the Lord of all the earth. (4:14) Oil is the symbol of the Holy Spirit. The olive tree is the symbol of Israel. The natural interpretation is that these two witnesses are Jews filled with the Spirit of God who shine forth the testimony of the Lord Jesus Christ.

5) As God's ambassadors, anyone who would harm them is attempting to harm God Himself. Their enemies are God's enemies, so they will be devoured by fire coming out of the mouths of the two witnesses. Our God is a consuming fire. (Hebrews 12:29 quoting Deuteronomy 4:24 which is quoted many times throughout the scriptures.) The shades of gray recede and the battle lines between good and evil grow clearer.

6) The plagues these men cause are not limited to Israel, or Egypt, but can be poured out on the entire earth. Drought, water turned to blood, and every kind of plague as often as they want. This is warfare intensifying. God wants men to repent, but refusal to do so will mean judgment. Life will no longer continue on as normal.

7) These witnesses are immortal until they finish their ministry. They were alive before the time of their testimony began, but it began on a certain day and lasted 1,260 days.

There are many beasts mentioned throughout Revelation. This beast is named as the beast that comes up from the abyss. He is the king of the locusts released by the 5th trumpet judgment, the first woe. He is the angel of the abyss whose name in Hebrew is Abaddon. (Rev. 9:11) The word beast in Revelation and Daniel, however, means a human government. The government of the antichrist will murder the two witnesses.

8-9) As a sign of the greatest possible disrespect, after killing these witnesses the beast leaves their bodies in the streets of Jerusalem for three and a half days. Jerusalem is called Sodom for materialism and sexual immortality. It is called Egypt for idolatry and spiritual immorality.

This is the only time in the book of Revelation where we can clearly point to modern technology, men from every people, tribe, language and nation will gaze on their bodies. Camera, newspapers, television films, movies and the internet all combine to make this possible.

10) They gloat because they are deluded into believing that they triumphed over God by murdering His ambassadors. The exchange of gifts shows both their great joy and how widespread is their delusion. Also we must remember that righteousness always torments the unrighteous. Even though very few suffered the direct judgments; the righteousness of these two witnesses torments the entire earth.

11) After three and one half days the Spirit of God blows on these two witnesses and they have the breath of life. The Greek word pneuma means spirit, breath and air. God breathed into Adam the breath of life. God's Spirit took Ezekiel to the valley of dry bones. Ezekiel prophesied; the four winds of heaven blew on them, the Spirit of God came and the wind of the air became the breath of life to the bones.

As Jonah was in the belly of the whale for three days and nights so Jesus was in the heart of the earth. After three and one half days, which proves that the beast actually killed them, they stand to their feet, very much alive. As everyone on earth views their death at the hands of the beast, so everyone on earth will view their resurrection. Not only does this testify to the power of God, but it also testifies to the defeat and ultimate destruction of the beast.

Refusing to repent, clinging to faith in the beast, the inhabitants of the earth witness their resurrection in terror. However, we have not been given the Spirit of fear, but of power and of love and of a sound mind. The same sight that terrifies those who rebel against our Savior gives us hope.

12) The great voice that calls the resurrected witnesses to heaven is another witness. Through modern technology all the earth will have the opportunity to see them ascend to heaven and disappear in a cloud. Once again, John shows that there is no middle ground. These people are not only unrepentant unbelievers. They are the enemies of God's witnesses. Unbelief makes the unbeliever God's enemy.

13) As the two witnesses ascend into the clouds, judgment falls on Jerusalem. A great earthquake destroys a tenth of Jerusalem, killing seven thousand. Those left alive in Jerusalem, though afraid, gave glory to the God of heaven.

14) The ascension of the two witnesses ends the second woe, which began with the sixth trumpet judgment. The two witnesses began their ministry 1,264 days earlier (1,260 + the 4 days their bodies lie in Jerusalem) in the middle of the tribulation, about the time the sacrifices were cut off and the abomination that causes desolation was set up.

The third woe comes without delay. Both possible meanings of the phrase comes quickly are probably true. There will be no delay and this woe will conclude rapidly.

15) When the seventh angel sounds his trumpet, John again sees the events of heaven first. This is the third and final woe. Under this judgment fall the seven bowl (KJV vial) judgments of chapter sixteen which conclude with the physical return of the Lord Jesus Christ to the earth.

The loud or great voices of heaven once again cause everyone to hear and be responsible for what is said. This claim of ownership of the earth is the theme of Handle's Hallelujah chorus. Though Christ has not yet returned, this claim is made at the sounding of the seventh trumpet. This is another reason I believe the third woe, which is the seventh trumpet judgment and includes all seven bowl judgments is very, very short, only a matter of days or at the most weeks. This praise, which points out that Jesus Christ will reign, emphasizes the promises repeated throughout the Word of God that this kingdom will never end.

16-18) The twenty-four elders, who represent the saints of all the ages, fall down in worship at this, the culmination of human history. Their praise begins with thanksgiving to God in a major change to the form John has used throughout Revelation, the One who is and who was. His coming is no longer future. Now He becomes simply the One who is and who was. By the third woe, the seventh trumpet judgment Jesus Christ begins to reign. This is the time that I believe the abomination that causes desolation is cleansed from the temple. This is the wrath of the lamb. The nations have hardened their own hearts and gather to war against the lamb.

Jesus Christ through His judgments is not responsible for destroying the earth. He destroys those unbelievers whose rebellion destroys the earth. Environmentalists who claim to love the earth are actually destroying the earth.

The time is at hand for rewarding those saints promised land through Abraham. However, the Great White Throne judgment is not for another thousand years. So the phrase the time has come for judging the dead must either refer to the spiritually dead being destroyed at Christ's coming or the word judge, krino, is being used in the unusual sense of rewarding the saints and prophets.

When Christ was crucified, He cried "It is finished," and the veil of the temple ripped in two from top to the bottom, showing that man had access to God. Now the ark in heaven is visible as God comes to the cleansed earth to claim His own. The flashes of lightning, rumblings, peals of thunder, an earthquake and a great hailstorm show God's power and holiness.

Chapter Twelve

v1) A great and wondrous sign appeared in heaven. This is the first time that a sign appears in Revelation. A mystery, like the seven stars and the lampstands in Chapter one, is something that has never been revealed to man before. Scientific reasoning cannot discover it. Everything else in Revelation assumes that the reader is familiar enough with the rest of the Word of God to understand the symbols, which have already been given.

For example, in Chapter One a sharp sword is coming out of the mouth of Jesus Christ. Paul has already told us in Ephesians 6:17 about the sword of the Spirit, which is the word of God. Therefore John expects us to know that this sword coming out of the mouth of Jesus Christ is the Word of God, the words of Jesus Christ.

Contrasting these already revealed symbols and newly revealed mysteries is this great sign in heaven. The miracles of Jesus were attesting signs, proofs of his deity. Paul's signatures were signs. This great sign in heaven then is a mighty, powerful symbol, which witnesses to the truth of everything else in Revelation. Since this is pointed out as a sign, everything else in Revelation should be interpreted either literally or according to clearly revealed symbols elsewhere in the Word of God.

Since it is in heaven, most believe that this sign will not be visible to those on the earth. It seems to me that this is a witness to the inhabitants of the earth. Verse 6 says that the woman will be taken care of for 1,260 days, so this sign takes place when the abomination which causes desolation is set up in the temple and the daily sacrifices are cut off at the beginning of the great tribulation. Maybe the great and wondrous sign will appear differently to those in heaven who see clearly, but I believe that the inhabitants of the earth will see this sign, even if it is unclear to them.

Since this is a sign, this woman cannot be Mary the mother of Jesus. Since the Church was not born until Pentecost, and this woman lives on earth during the great tribulation, this woman cannot be the Church. Since this woman gave birth to a male child, who will rule all the nations with an iron scepter, the Lord Jesus Christ, she must either be all believers throughout all the ages or she must be Israel. Since the promises of the Old Testament are that a Messiah would be given to Israel, I believe that this woman is Israel on earth. Clothed with the sun is the clothing of the splendor of heaven itself.

This emphasizes the glory, splendor and majesty with which God clothes His bride. The moon under her feet is the reflected glory of creation. Her crown of twelve stars is her authority to rule all creation while clothed in heaven's majesty. It shows Israel's actual position during the Millennium as administrating God's rule on earth.

v2) The birth of the Messiah was obvious to all who knew the Scriptures. Daniel prophesied the time of the Messiah's coming (Daniel 9:24-26) and Micah prophesied that the Messiah would be born in Bethlehem (Micah 5:2). This permitted Satan to unleash his unholy fury on the nation of Israel causing the labor pains for this woman that John saw in heaven.

vv3-4) Another sign appeared to John in heaven. The great red dragon is (v9) that old serpent, called the Devil and Satan. The stars are angels. In Revelation 1:20 the seven stars are a mystery which is revealed as the angels of the seven churches. In Job 38:7 the morning stars are angels. In Revelation 11:9 when Satan is cast out of heaven his angels are cast out with him.

Isaiah 1:18 calls our sins scarlet and crimson. Red, the color of blood, is the color of sin. This dragon is the symbol of evil. As the beast symbolizes both one world human government and the individual who heads that government, the antichrist, so the great red dragon symbolizes the hierarchy of fallen angels and demons headed by Satan. Seven is the number of divine or heavenly completion and ten is the number of earthly or material completion. There are ten commandments, ten plagues on Egypt, ten horns on the head of the fourth beast of Daniel chapter seven, the Roman Empire, and ten horns on the seven heads of the beast of Revelation 13.

A head on these beasts symbolizes the decision-making power, the actual person or government which is the head. A horn represents coercion, that is, police, military, taxation and legal powers. A crown represents royal or political power.

The tail is very much part of the dragon, but the opposite of those who actually make up the government. It is "below" the politicians, lawyers, policeman, soldiers, etc. It is the pressure and influence of "the little guy," the "ordinary citizen" on others. So Satan himself does not use any kind of physical or material force, but influences these angels. These angels choose to follow Satan.

The dragon understood the Word of God concerning the prophecies of the Christ. He made preparations for the Christ's destruction. This effort to devour the Christ was illustrated by Satan offering Christ all the kingdoms of the world if Christ would worship him.

v5) Despite the dragon's great effort, he fails. This male child can only be Jesus Christ, the enemy of the dragon. No other enemy of the dragon will rule all the nations with an iron scepter. The Christ will rule the nations without worshiping the dragon. Christ's death, burial and resurrection are portrayed as snatched up to God and to his throne. Christ's death was not his defeat, as the dragon thought, but his victory over the dragon.

Christ's victory over death makes physical death a victory for all believers.

v6) The child of the woman was snatched up to God more than sixty years before John wrote the book of Revelation. The woman, however, flees to a desert place during the great tribulation. No one knows the location of this place prepared for the woman. It is on earth for 1,260 days of the great tribulation. Since she is on earth and not in heaven, the woman is not the Church. I believe that this proves that the woman is Israel. This 1,260 days is 30 days less than the 1,290 days recorded by Daniel (12:11). Daniel records the time between the setting up of the abomination which causes desolation in the temple, breaking the covenant which allows temple sacrifices, and the seventh trumpet judgment. The 1,260 days probably begins after the setting up of the abomination which causes desolation and ends about the time of the sounding of the seventh trumpet judgment. As God miraculously provided for Elijah for three years during Israel's drought, so He will miraculously provide for Israel somewhere on earth out of the dragon's reach.

vv7-9) Today Satan is the Prince of the power of the air. He can, as he did to Job, go directly to God to accuse us. Satan will be forced out of heaven through warfare. We are not given the details of this war. God Himself does not fight against Satan directly, but Michael and his angels force the dragon and his angels out of heaven. We do not know the nature or weapons of their warfare, only the results.

That ancient serpent called the devil or Satan identifies the serpent of the Garden of Eden. From the beginning of the human race to its conclusion, we have been led astray. Everyone who wants to "do his own thing" is deluded, led astray by the one who leads the whole world astray.

Though we are not told when this war in heaven takes place, I believe that it begins sometime during the great tribulation and ends with the seventh trumpet judgment. Satan and his angels are thrown with force, hurled, to the earth. Satan is banished from heaven, God's throne. No one can be certain what hurled to the earth means. It could mean that Satan and his angels are simply limited to the surface of the earth, or it could mean that Satan and his angels are simply restricted to the material universe. Since he is now called the Prince of the Power of the Air it most likely means that Satan and his angels will be restricted to the surface of planet earth.

vv10-12) John hears a great voice in heaven proclaiming to those in all in heaven. There is no evidence that those on earth hear this proclamation. Since this is a result of the seventh trumpet, many believe that this war in heaven takes place throughout the great tribulation. I believe, however, that the time sequencing fits better with Satan being hurled from heaven before the abomination that causes desolation is set up in the temple.

The expulsion of Satan from heaven is proclaimed to be the fulfilling of salvation. This is not only our salvation, but also the salvation of the entire earth. The complete salvation of the material universe, however, must wait for the end of the Millennium. After the battle of Gog and Magog, after the Great White Throne judgment, the heavens will disappear with a roar; the elements will be destroyed by fire (II Peter 3:10) and God will create a new heaven and a new earth.

At this point in John's vision, however, the seventh trumpet signals the beginning of the seven bowl judgments which culminates with the battle of Armageddon.

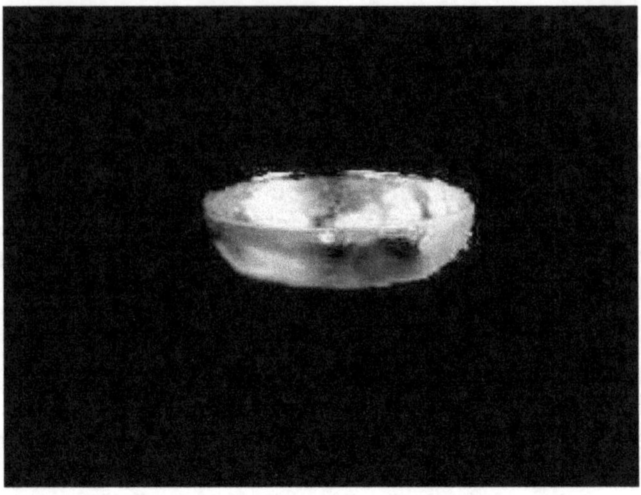

The salvation that the loud voice in heaven proclaims is not the "freedom" our American Establishment of Religion worships. It is the law of God enforced with a rod of iron throughout the entire earth. God is a God of love, and this act of love cleanses the earth by destroying all who will not bow the knee and worship Jesus Christ. Victory is proclaimed when the accuser is silenced. Though vv 7-9 say that Satan was hurled down by Michael and his angels, the victory proclamation names the weapons of Satan's defeat as the blood of the lamb, the word of their testimony and the willingness of believers to die for their faith.

Though the fall of Satan is the cause of great rejoicing in heaven, it is a great woe to the earth and to the sea. A woe is a curse of God. Satan understands the Scriptures but is blinded by his hatred of God and all that is His. Satan,

realizing that his time is short, still believes that he can defeat God.

vv 13-14) Unable to accuse us to God, Satan focuses on Israel, the woman. Repeating verse 6, John says that she goes to a place prepared for her in the desert. Because the woman was given the two wings of a great eagle so that she might fly to the place prepared for her, many modern commentators believe that this is some form of an airlift.

We have no information anywhere in the Word of God as to where this prepared place might be. All that we know is that it is in the desert. Exodus 19:4 uses the same image, that the children of Israel were carried ...on eagles wings when God miraculously provided for them during their travels in the Sinai desert. This does not mean that the place in the desert prepared for Israel during the tribulation is the Sinai desert again. It means that God once again will miraculously provide for Israel in the desert. There is no need to believe that these wings of a great eagle must be an airlift. The amount of time that God will miraculously provide for her, a time, times and half a time, is the same phrase Daniel uses for the great tribulation (Daniel 12:7), which is mentioned as 1,260 days in verse 6.

vv 15-16) Both the woman and the dragon are great signs. The water like a river and the earth swallowing the river are part of these signs. Jeremiah describes the armies of Nebuchadnezzar waters are rising and an overflowing torrent in 47:2. In 46:7& 8 Jeremiah says that Egypt rises like the Nile, like rivers of surging waters. This seems to indicate that the beast sends military forces after Israel. The physical earth could open up and swallow these forces as it swallowed up Korah and his followers (Numbers 16:31-33). If this happens, it would certainly be a sign to the inhabitants of the earth that God is protecting Israel.

v 17) This enrages Satan further. Those left alive on earth at this time who obey God's commandments and hold to the testimony of Jesus are the offspring of the woman, Israel. During the time of the Great Tribulation, faith in Jesus Christ is certain martyrdom.

Part Seven: Chapters Thirteen and Fourteen

Part Seven: Chapters Thirteen and Fourteen

Thirteen

v 1-2) Most Greek texts say he stood on the shore of the sea not and I stood on the shore of the sea. The difference between he, referring to the dragon, and I is just a single letter.

The dragon is a great sign, so these beasts are also signs. The dragon standing on the shore of the sea shows us that these beasts, though empowered by Satan, are not Satan himself. Otherwise, the two readings, I (John) or he (the dragon), have no effect on the interpretation of the rest of the chapter.

The sea continues the imagery of the river from Chapter 12. The river is military or paramilitary, while the sea is not controlled or disciplined like a river. It is the surging, restless sea of humanity. In Revelation 17:15 John describes the waters as peoples, multitudes, nations and languages. Daniel also sees a sea of humanity. In his vision, four beasts rise out of it. (Daniel 7:2,3) Babylon was a lion with the wings of an eagle. The Medes and the Persians were a bear. The Greeks were a leopard with four wings and four heads. Daniel sees the final beast, Rome, as terrifying and frightening and very powerful. It had large iron teeth; it crushed and devoured its victims and trampled underfoot whatever was left. It was different from all the former beasts and it had ten horns.

(Daniel 7:7) Each of the four beasts lived at different times and all ruled the Promised Land.

The beast that John saw resembled a leopard (Alexander the Great's Mesopotamian Greek Empire) and lives only during the tribulation. It has the feet of a bear (the Empire of the Medes and the Persians) and the mouth of a lion (the Babylonian Empire). The Medes and the Persians built the first empire-wide road system. The feet likely refer to a road/rail/air/sea transportation system. Nebuchadnezzar's Babylon had the first empire-wide communication system for the King to command his subjects. The mouth like a lion likely means communication, radio/internet/news-papers/magazines/television, at least from the antichrist to the people.

This beast cannot be Rome or a revived Roman Empire since Chapter 17:8 says that *the beast, which you saw, once was, now is not, and will come up out of the Abyss.* The Roman Empire existed in John's day. The beast is an Empire which existed before John, but did not exist in John's day.

Also, much time and energy have been wasted on attempts to determine the exact makeup of the beast, since both the heads and horns are various kings and kingdoms. They reign for one hour (17:12), so it will not be possible to know the exact make-up of the beast before it is revealed. Ten is the number of completion on earth; seven is the number of completion in heaven. Even if the numbers correspond to the exact number of kingdoms we will not know the exact kingdoms until they are revealed in the tribulation.

This beast has ten horns and seven heads with ten crowns on his horns. The dragon has ten horns, seven heads and seven crowns. The terrifying, frightening and very powerful fourth beast that Daniel saw had only one head with ten horns but no crowns. The scarlet beast, which the great prostitute of Revelation 17 sits on, has seven heads and ten horns. An angel tells John that each head is a king, each crown is a king and the beast itself is a king which belongs to the seven heads. Though there are no crowns on the Scarlet beast, it is the same beast that John sees here rising out of the sea. Here the beast is coming into existence. In Chapter 17 it has lost all of its royal dignity (no crowns) and is near the end of its existence. This beast has a blasphemous name on each head; the scarlet beast is covered in blasphemous names. The scarlet beast will come up out of the abyss and this beast has a head that seemed to have a fatal wound, but the fatal wound had been healed.

These beasts are kingdoms, but the beast thrown into the lake of fire at the return of Jesus Christ is just one person. So the beast is both an individual, the antichrist as head of a one-world government, and the kingdom of the whole world.

vv. 3-4) Satan must use a human, since he is a spiritual being, but this human comes up from the abyss and recovers from a fatal wound. Satan does not have the power to raise the dead. Many believe, therefore, that one of the heads seemed to have a fatal wound means that the beast will be the apparent restoration of a great kingdom of the past.

This belief goes on to say that the heads of the scarlet beast are described as seven kings and kings must have kingdoms. Human kingdoms do not rise from the abyss, but individuals can, as Samuel did for the witch at Endor (I Samuel 28). If this is an evil ruler risen from the dead, then who? Nebuchadnezzar? Hitler? The early church believed Nero because he was the first Roman Emperor to demand to be worshiped as god while he was alive. Before Nero, Emperor worship was a form of ancestor worship. The head of this beast with a fatal wound that is healed, however, seems to be a kingdom. The answer is a human king rising from the abyss that amazes the entire world by bringing an ancient kingdom back into existence.

These "resurrections" astonish all who refuse to believe the truth. This is part of what Paul calls a powerful delusion so that they will believe the lie. (II Thessalonians 2:11) This powerful delusion will cause them to follow the beast. This leads to direct worship of the dragon and the beast. They will worship Satan believing that the Dragon and the beast are more powerful than God. The question *Who is like the beast?* shows that these deluded rebels believe that there is no other spiritual being with the power or authority of the dragon. They either believe that there is no god or that god is less powerful than the dragon. Who can make war against the beast? They believe that there is no power in heaven or earth as powerful as the beast. Some people even understand the coming war against heaven and are deluded into believing that they can win.

vv. 5-6) This mouth of the beast is more than the mouth which everyone has. It is the ability to deliver these proud words and blasphemies, a control of the mass media.

The 42 months of the beast's authority is the Great Tribulation. Once again, the beginning point is the breaking of the covenant by stopping the sacrifices and setting up the abomination that causes desolation in the temple.

vv. 7-9) Though the dragon has been hurled from heaven, he will have vast, almost unlimited power on earth at this time which he gives to the beast. During the Great Tribulation there will be saints on earth. These were unbelievers at the time of the rapture who have since had their names written in the Lamb's book of life. The beast will make war against them and conquer them. THE BEAST WILL NOT TOLERATE ANYONE WHO REFUSES TO WORSHIP HIM. At this time, there will no longer be any shades of gray. Righteousness is a death sentence. All inhabitants of the earth, except these young believers, will worship the beast.

He who has an ear to hear, let him hear. This is not only eternal life, but physical life as well. Anyone who listens and repents before the return of Christ for His Church will not have to be conquered by the beast.

v 10) Saints at this time are predestined for either the sword or captivity. Being a true believer will call for more patient endurance and faithfulness at that time than we at this time must endure.

vv 11-17) This second beast is the false prophet of Revelation 16:13 & 19:20. He completes the unholy trinity.

The dragon is the counterfeit God the Father, the beast counterfeits God the Son and this second beast counterfeits God the Holy Spirit. The first beast is a one-world government headed by the antichrist. One head seemed to have had a fatal wound that was healed. The beast itself will come up out of the abyss. The second beast, however, which is the false prophet, will come out of the earth. The earth, contrasting the sea where the first beast comes from, can mean the stability of human government. But the phrase coming out of the earth is found in I Samuel 28:13 when the witch of Endor said to Saul "I see a spirit coming up out of the ground." This second beast is more than just empowered from the Abyss; he himself comes out of the ground.

He looks harmless. Though he has two horns, they are like a lamb. The horns of a lamb are nothing more than two very small nubs. His military power is weak, ceremonial. The traditional Reformed position is that this is the Papacy with its Swiss honor guard. His speech is empowered by the dragon. As Jesus said, "By their fruit you will recognize them." (Matthew 7:16) Like all beasts in the Word of God, this is both an organization and an individual who heads the organization.

The works of the false prophet will be to use the authority of the beast to make the earth and its inhabitants worship the first beast. Forcing people to worship the abomination that causes desolation, the image of the antichrist set up in the temple seems like the madness of Nero or a thousand other tyrants. But inanimate objects and animals are unable to worship anything. The false prophet dedicates and uses the entire earth in this worship of the beast. But the earth here is likely used in the same way as the beast that came out of the earth, what we would call the underworld.

The false prophet works his lying wonders during the ministry of God's two witnesses. Jannes and Jambres opposed Moses by copying some of the Lord's signs (II Timothy 3:8), so the false prophet will be able to call down fire from heaven. He will be able to do anything necessary to deceive the inhabitants of the earth, including bringing spirit, breath, wind to a lifeless idol and making it speak.

The most convincing sign, however, is the healing of the fatal wound. This counterfeit resurrection is the foundation for this new religion. Mystical religions, such as Hinduism, the New Age Movement and Wicca, will have no difficulty adding one more god. Secular humanists will be awed by supernatural events which defy pure material explanations. As the miracles of Jesus were signs, so these great miracles are signs to deceive.

Thousands have testified to hearing lifeless idols speak in this age. This image of the beast will go beyond this, however, and cause all who refuse to worship the image to be killed. Nebuchadnezzar foreshadowed this by making an image of himself and killing everyone who refused to worship it. And as God preserved Shadrach, Meshech and Abednego, so the Lord Jesus Christ will preserve a remnant who refuse to worship the beast.

The greatest crime of the twenty-first century is identity theft. To counter this it is claimed that we need a national ID card. But national identification does not work across national borders. Besides, cards can still be forged. The proposed answer to this is a permanent identification as part of a person. With this positive, unforgeable ID, all money would become electronic.

Every financial transaction would be through a central database. These are not proposals for the great tribulation, but for the near future in North America, Japan, Europe and China. Even unbelievers see the danger of allowing someone to control such a database.

The Word of God only says that some sort of ID mark will be required to buy or sell. It says nothing about database. The beast is only interested in forcing everyone to worship him so the required ID mark will be a visible, public sign with the same purpose as the Romans had with the annual burning of a pinch of incense to an image of Caesar.

The final system of buying and selling which the false prophet forces on everyone in the name of the beast might be nothing that we can even dream of today. The beast is not interested in the means, only in forcing the inhabitants of the earth to worship him by receiving his mark. Once again this is a counterfeit. The seal of God is at this time on the foreheads of the 144,000. Also, not everyone on earth will receive the mark of the beast. They who refuse the mark of the beast will pay with their physical lives (Revelation 20:4).

vv 17b-18) The mark of the beast is the name of the beast or the number of his name. This calls for wisdom. This is the wisdom which Solomon repeatedly pleaded with us to get.

Wisdom is supreme; therefore get wisdom.
Though it cost all you have, get understanding.
Proverbs 4:7

This wisdom is more like what we think of as skill. In this case, skill in knowing and correctly applying the Word of God, directed by the Spirit of God; one who correctly handles the Word of God (II Timothy 2:15).

Six is the number of man, three the number of god. While 666 is certainly man proclaiming himself to be god, there is more. The Greek word for six is pronounced as "hex" in English. The Greek also spells out six hundred sixty-six, to leave no doubt as to the exact number. Also, for it is man's number, meaning all mankind, could be translated "for it is the number of a man" (KJV) meaning the Antichrist. The mark of the beast has power in and of itself. Those slain for Jesus during the Great Tribulation will be victorious over the beast and his image and over the number of his name (Revelation 15:2). At this time we cannot know the exact mark of beast. It will be revealed during the tribulation.

Chapter Fourteen

vv. 1-5) These are the same 144,000 Jewish males, 12,000 from each tribe, that were sealed in Chapter 7. Now John reveals that this seal is the Lamb's Name and His Father's Name.

Chapter 13 ended with the inhabitants of the Earth forced to take the mark of the beast. This is near the middle of the tribulation, that is, the beginning of the Great Tribulation.

Verse 14 of this chapter is the very end of the Great Tribulation. I believe that this entire chapter belongs together, making this near the battle of Armageddon.

Mount Zion is Jerusalem. It is only a small part of the Temple area and the city of David. There would be little room left for anyone else on Mount Zion. They are with Jesus Christ where ever he goes, before the throne, and before the four living creatures and the elders. They had been redeemed from the Earth. These comments make some conclude that the 144,000 are martyred and that this entire scene is in heaven. They interpret Mount Zion in the sense of Hebrews 12:12, as the heavenly Jerusalem.

Others believe that Mount Zion is the Temple area of Jerusalem here on Earth and that before the throne is the same as *Let us boldly approach the throne of grace.* (Hebrews 4:16) The throne of grace is clearly in heaven while we are on Earth. I believe that this is the period of the cleansing of the Temple from the Abomination that causes Desolation. It is after the seventh trumpet but before Jesus Christ touches his feet to the Mount of Olives. I believe that this is the preparation for the return of God's presence in the Temple, the returning Shekinah glory. This will be a tremendous struggle in both heaven and Earth. This passage simply explains the purity of these men.

Their purity is their power. God is holy and cannot dwell in the presence of sin. As the tribe of Levi was offered to God in place of the firstborn of all Israel, so these men are the first fruits from among men. They live in the presence of the resurrected Christ, who is their power.

Only their sexual purity and their integrity are mentioned. Above all else, guard your heart, for it is the wellspring of life. (Proverbs 4:23).

No lie was found in their mouths; they are blameless. (Revelation 14: 5)

vv. 6-13) Immediately before the harvest of the Earth, the war of Armageddon, three angels announce God's final message to those who live on the Earth--to every nation, tribe, language, and people. This is near the end of the ministry of the two witnesses.

The first angel flies in midair, the atmosphere. To everyone on Earth he proclaims the eternal gospel. God will hold every single individual on Earth responsible for what he says.

At this time, just before the sounding of the seventh trumpet, the beast has silenced every other witness. The woman, Israel, is miraculously provided for in the desert. The 144,000 are with the Lamb. All others who refused to worship the beast have been martyred. So God provides his own witnesses.

As in Galatians 1:8 and I Cor. 15:1, the word for preach or proclaims is the noun and verb forms of the same Greek word as gospel. In Galatians, Paul proclaims damnation to anyone who proclaims a different gospel. I Cor. 15 defines the gospel as the death, burial and resurrection of Jesus Christ according to the Scriptures. This seems to be a different gospel.

At this time on Earth, the beast and the false prophet are busy forcing everyone to battle against God in Armageddon in northern Israel. Instead of countering all of the Satanic deceit which drives men to worship and obey the beast, this angel simply proclaims Jesus Christ as creator, the only one who is to be worshiped. At this time it is as simple a message as possible. Obeying this gospel will bring immediate martyrdom.

The four things mentioned, the heavens, the Earth, the sea, and the springs of water are the sources of life.

The message of the second angel, *Fallen! Fallen is Babylon the great*, is used by cults all over the world. These cults apply the label Babylon to true Christianity. The message is clear: Babylon is the self-indulgent religion of the Dragon. It is both spiritual and economic. Some are deceived by the Dragon into believing that the Dragon is God. Others are seduced by her sinful pleasures. It will encompass all other religions on Earth during the great tribulation.

Though the message of the first angel is difficult to reconcile with the message of the gospel that Paul preaches, the message of the third angel is even more difficult to accept. Everyone still alive, except Israel, the 144,000, and the two witnesses, have the mark of the beast. The message of the third angel seems to say that everyone else on Earth is damned already. Hebrews 10:26 says, if we deliberately keep on sinning after we have received the knowledge of the truth, no sacrifice for sins is left, but only a fearful expectation of judgment in raging fire. My question is, why would this angel proclaim this message if everyone on Earth is past hope? Perhaps the mark of the beast can be removed.

The final message is a voice from heaven. This voice seems to be only for John. There is nothing which says that anyone else on Earth hears it. It proclaims with certainty that others will die for the name of Jesus. It also proclaims a change in dispensations. The resurrected church becomes part of the armies of heaven. Those who die in Jesus from this point onward go to immediate rest.

vv. 14-20) These verses show the end of the Great Tribulation. Chapter 15 to the middle of 19 all describe events which take place before this final harvest of the Earth.

The Son of Man is a title of Jesus Christ in both Daniel 7:13 and throughout the Gospels, especially Mark. His crown is the victor's crown. Though He is ruler of all, He submits to His father's will. These angels fulfill what Jesus prophesied in Matthew 24:36, that even the Son does not know the day or hour: only the Father in heaven knows.

Blood is a liquid which dries rapidly. For blood to flow, rising as high as the horses' bridles for a distance of about 180 miles, it must be a swift destruction. This is outside the city. The entire length of Israel is about 180 miles. The valley of Armageddon to Jerusalem is only about 50 miles.

Part Eight: Chapters 15-16

Part Eight: Chapters 15-16

Chapter Fifteen

v. 1) Once again John is in heaven, viewing another great and marvelous sign. This tells us that no one on earth will see the events recorded in this chapter. These final seven judgments will be completed in days; at the most, weeks. When they are completed, the earth will be cleansed of sin and a thrice holy God will come down to dwell with men.

vv. 2-4) John also sees the crystal sea mixed with fire this time. Fire is both judgment and purification. The sea of glass is heaven's "view port" of earth from heaven, so the great sign of fire is not the final judgment Peter writes about where the elements melt. This fire is the final seven judgments leading up to and including the battle of Armageddon. The throne behind the sea of glass in chapter 4 is not mentioned here so the Lord God Almighty is no longer seated. He is personally involved in these final judgments.

Those victorious over the beast stand around the sea, viewing the final judgment of the earth. They are victorious not only over the beast and his image, but also over the number of his name. These refused to take the mark of the beast and their victory is their martyrdom.

As they surround the crystal sea mixed with fire, they worship the Lord God Almighty, the just, true and holy creator. But all who refuse to worship the Lamb suffer the judgment of eternal damnation proclaimed by the third angel in chapter 14.

Only those redeemed through martyrdom from the Great Tribulation are mentioned as singing at this time. The Scriptures do not say that we will be singing at this time.

Their harps might symbolize musical instruments in general, or they might represent any kind of stringed instruments, or it might mean simply harps. We know that this is the time for the victorious believers to sing praise. The song of Moses which they sing is either Exodus 15 or Deuteronomy 32. Perhaps it is both.

The song of the Lamb, as recorded here, proclaims Jesus Christ as King of the Earth with all nations worshiping Him. No longer are these martyrs asking how long. This is the day of their vindication.

vv. 5-8) The Testimony John saw was foreshadowed by both the Tabernacle of Moses and Solomon's Temple. Exodus 34:29 calls the two stone tablets which Moses carved into the Ten Commandments the two tablets of the testimony. The Lord calls them simply the Testimony in Exodus 16:34. They were placed in the Ark of the Covenant, as recorded in Exodus 25:16, 21. When the Testimony was placed in the ark (Exodus 25:22), the ark became the ark of the Testimony. Because the Testimony was inside the ark, which was inside the tabernacle, the entire tabernacle became the tent of the Testimony, Numbers 17:4,7, 8.

John sees that the temple, that is, the tabernacle of the testimony was opened. Heaven opened, the temple opened, the Holy of Holies opened, and the ark opened, which revealed the Testimony. Our God is a consuming fire, a holy God which cannot dwell in the presence of sin.

The seven angels are dressed as priests performing the act of sacrifice. The fire in the sea of glass is the altar.

The unrepentant wicked of the earth are both judged for their sin and offered as sacrifice to cleanse the earth of sin as the Lord God almighty comes to dwell on earth.

Both the tabernacle of Moses and the temple of Solomon were filled with the glory of the Lord at their dedication so that no one could enter to minister. Exodus 40:33, 34 and I Kings 8:10, 11. This temple in heaven will be filled with smoke, as in Isaiah's vision of the temple (Isaiah 6:4), until the earth is cleansed from sin and the glory of God can once again dwell in His temple on earth.

Chapter Sixteen

v. 1) The loud voice from the temple commanding the angels to pour out their plagues on the earth is the voice of the Lord God Almighty. This ends the signs in heaven and begins the visible plagues on the earth. Some commentators believe that these seven bowl judgments are the heavenly view of the seven trumpet judgments. Most, however, believe that these seven bowl judgments happen after the blowing of the seventh trumpet.

v. 2) The first bowl judgment is poured out on the land, and ugly and painful sores broke out on people. In the first trumpet judgment (Revelation 8:7) there came hail and fire mixed with blood, and it was hurled down upon the earth. A third of the earth was burned up, a third of the trees were burned up, and all the green grass was burned up.

Both of these are plagues on the land. The trumpet judgment is on a third of the land, while the bowl judgment is on everyone who has the mark of the beast.

v. 3) The second bowl judgment is poured out on the sea, and it turned into blood like that of a dead man, and every living thing in the sea died. In the second trumpet judgment (Revelation 8:8,9) something like a huge mountain, all ablaze, was thrown into the sea. A third of the sea turned into blood, a third of the living creatures in the sea died, and a third of the ships were destroyed.

Both of these are plagues on the sea. The trumpet judgment, which is presented first, says that only a third of the living creatures in the sea died. The bowl judgment says that every living thing in the sea died.

vv. 4-7) The third bowl judgment is poured out on the rivers and springs of water, and they became blood. In the third trumpet judgment (Revelation 8:10,11) a great star, blazing like a torch, fell from the sky on a third of the rivers and on the springs of water-- the name of the star is Wormwood. A third of the waters turned bitter, and many people died from the waters that had become bitter.

Both of these are plagues on the rivers and springs of water. The trumpet judgment has a third of the fresh water becoming poisonous, while the bowl judgment has all fresh water on earth turning to blood.

vv. 8-9) The fourth bowl judgment is poured out on the sun, and the sun was given power to scorch people with fire. They were seared by the intense heat and they cursed the name of God, who had control over these plagues, but they refused to repent and glorify him. In the fourth trumpet judgment (Revelation 8:12) a third of the sun was struck, a third of the moon, and a third of the stars, so that a third of them turned dark. A third of the day was without light, and also a third of the night.

Both of these are plagues on the sun. The trumpet judgment is on a third of the sun, moon and stars, while the bowl judgment increases the heat of the sun on the entire earth.

vv. 10-11) The fifth bowl judgment is poured out on the throne of the beast, and his kingdom was plunged into darkness. Men gnawed their tongues in agony and cursed the God of heaven because of their pains and their sores, but they refused to repent of what they had done. In the fifth trumpet judgment (Revelation 9:1) John saw a star that had fallen from the sky to the earth. The star was given the key to the shaft of the Abyss.

Both of these are plagues on the Kingdom of the beast, causing intense pain to those who worship the beast. The trumpet judgment is five months long. It releases evil creatures from the Abyss onto the earth to torment the entire earth. The bowl judgment is a direct judgment from heaven.

vv. 12-14) The sixth bowl judgment is poured out on the great river Euphrates, and its water was dried up to prepare the way for the kings from the East. In the sixth trumpet judgment (Revelation 9:13) the four angels who are bound at the great river Euphrates are released.

Both of these are plagues on the Euphrates River to dry it up to allow invading armies to come from the East. The trumpet judgment describes the armies which come to fight God at Armageddon while the bowl judgment describes the demonic trinity which seduces the leaders of the earth to fight God at Armageddon.

v 15) Seiss believes that this clothing which Jesus mentions at this time is the righteousness of belief in Christ resulting in another resurrection at this time. The nakedness is unbelief resulting in damnation.

vv. 16-21) The seventh bowl judgment is poured out into the air to the words It is done. In the seventh trumpet judgment (Revelation 11:15) loud voices proclaim “The kingdom of the world has become the kingdom of our

Lord and of his Christ, and he will reign for ever and ever." The seventh trumpet judgment is the prophesied trump of God throughout the Old Testament.

Both of these proclaim the immediate return of the Lord Jesus Christ to set up His Kingdom on Earth.

If these bowl judgments are another view of the trumpet judgments, then the sixth trumpet judgment, the drying up of the Euphrates river will not be repeated under the sixth bowl judgment. This is sensible, however, the fourth judgment does not line up as well. The end of the sixth bowl judgment mentions the gathering of the nations at Armageddon. The sixth trumpet judgment is the gathering of an army of two hundred million in Israel, though the exact place is not mentioned.

This is time of the Battle of Armageddon, the fall of Babylon, the most destructive earthquake the world has ever known, hailstones about one hundred pounds each and Jerusalem splitting into three parts. These final events happen within days or even hours of each other.

All mountains will be leveled, all cities except Jerusalem leveled, islands displaced and the earth will have a new climate which will restore our lifespan. As Isaiah says

he who dies at a hundred
will be thought a mere youth;
he who fails to reach a hundred
will be considered accursed.

Unrepentant mankind, however, cursed God ... because the plague was so terrible.

Part Nine: Chapters Seventeen, Eighteen and Nineteen

Part Nine: Chapters Seventeen, Eighteen, and Nineteen

Chapter Seventeen

A Tale Of Two Cities

From the Fall, Satan has attacked true religion. True religion is the pure virgin, Jerusalem. The Satanic counterfeit is the great prostitute, Babylon.

vv 1-6) One of the seven angels who had the seven bowls came and said to me...

The last trumpet has sounded and the final bowl judgment is poured out. John sees a vision of a woman on the beast during the battle, or more accurately the war, of Armageddon. She is judged at the same time as the beast, hours or days before the return of Jesus Christ when His feet touch the Mount of Olives.

Like every prostitute, this great prostitute who sits on many waters sincerely believes that she will never be judged. In Lev 20:10, God's Law commands that both the adulterer and the adulteress be put to death. The adulterers are the kings of the earth. Verse seventeen says that the many waters the prostitute sits on are the inhabitants of the earth. She seduces them as well as the kings.

Her story begins with the protoevangelium, Genesis 3:15.

And I will put enmity
between you and the woman,
and between your offspring and hers;
he will crush your head,
and you will strike his heel.

God's promise to the offspring of the woman is found in corrupted form in every ancient religion in the world. Western culture is most familiar which the heroic myth Achilles. Achilles, as with any Satanic deception, changes the ending. Instead of the non-fatal blow promised by the Lord, the blow to Achilles heel destroys him and Achilles never crushes the serpent's head. As with all ancient mythology, Achilles corrupts the Lord's promises. It combines the Lord's revealed promises with Satanic deceptions that make the beast the ultimate victor.

In Genesis 6:4 we read that the Nephilim were on the earth in those days--and also afterward--when the sons of God went to the daughters of men and had children by them. They were the heroes of old, men of renown.

The Hebrew word translated as heroes is the same word used to describe Nimrod, the son of Cush, grandson of Ham, great-grandson of Noah. Since Noah lived 350 years after the flood, Noah probably lived to see Nimrod, the mighty warrior on the earth. He was a mighty hunter before the LORD; that is why it is said, "Like Nimrod, a mighty hunter before the LORD." The first centers of his kingdom were Babylon, Erech, Akkad and Calneh, in Shinar. From that land he went to Assyria, where he built Nineveh, Rehoboth Ir, Calah and Resen, which is between Nineveh and Calah; that is the great city. Genesis 10.

J.A. Seiss says, "The Targum of Jonathan (a Jewish commentary on the Old Testament) interprets this to mean that he was a mighty rebel before the Lord, the mightiest rebel before the Lord that ever was in the earth. The Jerusalem Targum reads it that he was mighty in sin before the Lord, a hunter of the sons of men, exhorting them to leave the judgments of Shem and adhere to the judgments of Nimrod."

Idolatry began suddenly with Nimrod. He built a tower at "his first and capital city Bab-el, which, in the language of the time, means The Gate of God." (Seiss, p. 389) When the Lord confounds the languages, Nimrod's idolatrous Bab-el, the Gate of God becomes Babel, confusion, the true meaning of idolatry. Babylon is man in sinful rebellion attempting to become God. Every religion ever devised by man began in this city of Nimrod, Babylon. Babylon is both a city on the Euphrates River and man's clenched fist in the face of the Lord God Almighty by worship of false gods. Babylon includes Taoism, Confucianism, Shamanism, Islam, Hinduism, Mormonism, Shintoism and every other false religion on earth.

Many prophets prophesied the fall of the city of Babylon. For example, Isaiah prophesied in Isa 13:19-22

Babylon, the jewel of kingdoms,
the glory of the Babylonians' pride,
will be overthrown by God
like Sodom and Gomorrah.
She will never be inhabited
or lived in through all generations;
no Arab will pitch his tent there,
no shepherd will rest his flocks there.
But desert creatures will lie there,
jackals will fill her houses;
there the owls will dwell,
and there the wild goats will leap about.
Hyenas will howl in her strongholds,
jackals in her luxurious palaces.
Her time is at hand,
and her days will not be prolonged.

When the Chaldean empire of Nebuchadnezzar fell to the Medo-Persians, the city of Babylon became a great provincial capital. When the Persian Empire fell to Alexander the Great, Babylon was Alexander's vision for the capital of his entire empire. Babylon has never been overthrown by God like Sodom and Gomorrah.

Zechariah saw a vision, which prophesied Babylon as a great center of commerce. He had an angel show him a vision. Zechariah asked, "What is it?"

He (the angel) replied, "It is a measuring basket." And he added, "This is the iniquity of the people throughout the land." Then the cover of lead was raised, and there in the basket sat a woman! He said, "This is wickedness," and he pushed her back into the basket and pushed the lead cover down over its mouth. Then I looked up--and there before me were two women, with the wind in their wings! They had wings like those of a stork, and they lifted up the basket between heaven and earth. "Where are they taking the basket?" I asked the angel who was speaking to me. He replied, "To the country of Babylonia to build a house for it. When it is ready, the basket will be set there in its place."

The measuring basket Zechariah saw is commerce, the woman of iniquity is the same as Babylon, which John saw. Zechariah lived after Ezra led the people of Israel back to the land of Israel. The second temple was rebuilt. Babylon was in decline. Sometime in the future, according to this vision of Zechariah, Babylonia will be the world center of commerce.

The Babylon John sees is both a city on the Euphrates River, the commercial capital of the world, and every form of religious idolatry, which rejects the true God of Heaven. Her garments, jewelry and golden cup are the glitter of the outward trappings of religion. The cup is filled with the filth of the actual practices of religion. The mystery, something that can only be known by direct revelation from God, is the revelation of the unity of all false religions, from the grossest paganism to good sounding apostate Protestantism. All prostitution, physical and spiritual, are some form of rebellion against the Lord God Almighty.

The scarlet covered beast on which she rides is the same beast John saw rise out of the sea in Chapter 13. Chapter 13 shows the beginning of the life of this beast. This is three and a half years later near its end. It began life looking like a leopard. Now it is scarlet (the color of sin) and filled with names of blasphemies. For over three years it has martyred anyone who refused to accept its mark or worship its image. The Harlot, however, has martyred those who bore the testimony of Jesus since Nimrod's Babylon.

vv 7-18) When the angel guiding John explains the mystery to John, he begins with the beast. The beast, which you saw, once was, now is not, and will come up out of the Abyss and go to his destruction. Also in verse 11 The beast who once was, and now is not, is an eighth king. He belongs to the seven and is going to his destruction. The seven mountains are kingdoms, each headed by a kingdom and the seven heads are historic kingdoms. The angel guiding John explains this. They are also seven kings. Five have fallen, one is, the other has not yet come.

So the seven heads are also seven mountains, which are seven kingdoms. While they are not identified exactly, five kingdoms no longer existed in John's day, one existed in John's day and one was still future to John. The kingdom in John's day was Rome. Most commentators believe that the three kingdoms revealed to Daniel are earlier of the earlier kingdoms; Babylon, Medo-Persia and Greece. There is less agreement about the two kingdoms prior to Nebuchadnezzar's Babylon (the Chaldean Empire). The possible empires are Nimrod's Babylon, the Assyrian and the Egyptian. The important kingdom is the one that is future. This will be the one world government of the Anti-Christ. It will be one of the earlier kingdoms and will now rule over all the other kingdoms.

The ten horns you saw are ten kings who have not yet received a kingdom, but who for one hour will receive authority as kings along with the beast. They have one purpose and will give their power and authority to the beast.

We are not told anything else about these rulers. Horns represent military power and coercion, such as taxation. At the time of the end, however, they will be clearly revealed.

The beast will hate any other form of religion. He will destroy any sanctuary, temple, article, statue, book or anything else used to worship anyone or anything other than himself.

This chapter closes with "The woman you saw is the great city that rules over the kings of the earth." Babylon is a religious system. It is also a city on the Euphrates River, which will once again rise to power and seduce the entire world.

Chapter Eighteen

Chapter Seventeen's vision was given to John so that John could give it to the Church. The angel in Chapter Eighteen is a different angel. This angel's message is for the inhabitants of the earth at the end of the great tribulation. John, representing the entire Church, is simply an observer of this message.

v 1) When this angel comes down from heaven the entire earth will be illuminated by his splendor.

Habakkuk said of the LORD:

His glory covered the heavens
and his praise filled the earth.
His splendor was like the sunrise;
rays flashed from his hand,
where his power was hidden.
Plague went before him;
pestilence followed his steps.
He stood, and shook the earth;
he looked, and made the nations tremble.
The ancient mountains crumbled
and the age-old hills collapsed.
His ways are eternal.
And Isaiah said:

Go into the rocks,
hide in the ground
from dread of the LORD
and the splendor of his majesty!
The eyes of the arrogant man will be humbled
and the pride of men brought low;
the LORD alone will be exalted in that day.
The LORD Almighty has a day in store
for all the proud and lofty,
for all that is exalted
(and they will be humbled),
for all the cedars of Lebanon, tall and lofty,
and all the oaks of Bashan,
for all the towering mountains
and all the high hills,

for every lofty tower
and every fortified wall,
for every trading ship
and every stately vessel.
The arrogance of man will be brought low
and the pride of men humbled;
the LORD alone will be exalted in that day,
and the idols will totally disappear.
Men will flee to caves in the rocks
and to holes in the ground
from dread of the LORD
and the splendor of his majesty,
when he rises to shake the earth.

No created being can illuminate the entire earth with his glory, majesty, and splendor. This is the return of the Lord Jesus Christ Himself. The Son pronounces the judgment ("The Father judges no one, but has entrusted all judgment to the Son" John 5:22). Beginning with verse 4, the Holy Spirit offers one final audible invitation.

vv 2-3) Once again, a great shout is given, making the inhabitants of the earth responsible for their decisions. Fallen is called out twice, once for the religious idolatry of Nimrod's Babylon and once for the city of commerce on the Euphrates river. She is condemned to be an eternal dwelling place of demons, every evil spirit and every detestable bird. She is judged for her spiritual adulteries, idolatry, and her material adulteries, covetousness.

Her adulteries are called a maddening wine. Like all adultery, the adulterers become intoxicated with their sin. The nations drank her wine. The nations are both the governmental authorities and the people who make up individual nations. The kings of the earth committed adultery with her. Perhaps the peoples who make up the nations of the earth did not understand what they were doing. They are simply drunk from her maddening wine.

Their leaders, however, the kings of the earth, know and willfully choose to rebel against the Lord God Almighty. Also, the merchants of the earth grew rich from her excessive luxuries. These men seem to be Atheists, at least in practice. These covetous men worship their own appetites. Paul describes them in Philippians 3:19 as men whose end is destruction, whose god is their appetite, and whose glory is in their shame, who set their minds on earthly things. (NASB) Like the rioting silversmiths in Ephesus, these men disguise their greed by claiming religious devotion. The truth is, these men care nothing for the lives of others.

vv 4-8) Just before the final return of the Lord Jesus Christ in judgment to end the great tribulation and set up his personal reign where he will rule with a rod of iron, the Holy Spirit cries out with one final invitation. *Come out of her, my people*. This is the very end of the seventieth week of Daniel, and some people that God calls my people, still live in Babylon! Surely this must be the commercial city of Babylon and not participants in her pagan worship! If they refuse to listen, if they insist on remaining in the physical city of Babylon, they will share in the physical judgments on the physical city. Babylon will be consumed by fire. For the persecution of God's saints since Nimrod, God will give back to her as she has given; pay her back double for what she has done. Mix her a double portion from her own cup. Her judgment is to receive what she has given to others. And she is completely deluded into believing that she will never be judged for her sins.

Jeremiah prophesied:

"Flee from Babylon!
Run for your lives!
Do not be destroyed because of her sins.
It is time for the LORD's vengeance;
he will pay her what she deserves.
Babylon was a gold cup in the LORD's hand;
she made the whole earth drunk.
The nations drank her wine;
therefore they have now gone mad.

This Revelation given to John is a promised blessing to all who read, hear and take to heart what is written in it. (Rev 1:3) These judgments are not written to depress us, but to glorify the God of Heaven. All who boast that they will never mourn for their sins are condemned, even now.

God says of Babylon, her sins are piled up. He calls her sins crimes and says that Babylon will receive judgment from her own cup. Liberals claim that God is harsh in his judgments. But God says 'Give her as much torture and grief as the glory and luxury she gave herself.' Liberals claim that torture and grief are unfair and unjust. But God's Word says mighty is the Lord God who judges

Babylon. The plagues, death, mourning and famine are the judgments of a just and holy God.

vv 9-19) God does not want anyone to perish, but everyone to come to repentance (2 Peter 3:9). Yet the judgment of Babylon hardens the hearts of her lovers, the kings of the earth. Once again, they refuse to repent. Instead of seeing the justice of a loving God, they selfishly cry over their own losses, no one buys their cargoes any more. This lengthy list of Babylon's luxuries is not intended to be complete. Babylon has everything the human heart desires, but it all vanishes like a vapor while the kings of the earth can do nothing but cry out 'Woe, woe!' They express no voice of concern for the lost souls but only cry out in selfishness for their lost markets.

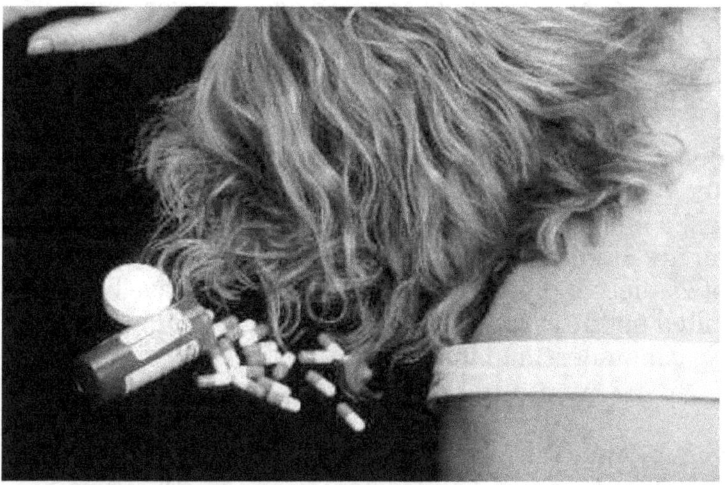

The last item on the list of her merchandise is the bodies and souls of men. While this is slavery, it is more than slavery. This includes drug addiction, prostitution, welfare, gambling, drunkenness and every other tool of Satan to snare the souls of men.

They claim Babylon the greatest city that ever existed while the truth is that she is a rebellious counterfeit of the holy city the New Jerusalem. They repeatedly mourn that Babylon was destroyed in one hour. One hour does not mean sixty minutes like we mean. It simply means very rapidly.

vv 20-24) The judgment of Babylon for the saints is a time of rejoicing, however. While the kings of the earth weep and bemoan her fall, we will rejoice! Rejoice over her, O heaven! Rejoice saints and apostles and prophets!

The millstone cast into the sea, the punishment for anyone who causes a little child who believes in Jesus to sin, shows how rapidly and violently Babylon's destruction will come. The city of music, commerce and social activity will end. The temporary mirth of Babylon will be replaced by the eternal joy of Jerusalem. The season for the pleasures of sin is eternally ended.

Six times the phrase never heard again, never found again, never shine again or not ever found again is used. We rejoice because Babylon is destroyed, never again to use her magic spell to lead all the nations astray.

In her was found the blood of prophets and of the saints, and of all who have been killed on the earth. This is not just a judgment on the men alive in the city of Babylon on the Euphrates River at the end of the seventieth week of Daniel. God judges Babylon for all who have been killed on the earth. There is more to this judgment than we can understand in this life.

Chapter Nineteen

vv 1-5) After the fall of Babylon, the hour that brought Babylon to ruin and ended her joy and mirth eternally, John heard what sounded like the roar of a great multitude in heaven shouting. We are not told if this multitude includes the Church, all believers, Israel, those redeemed from out of the tribulation, angels or other beings we now know nothing about. Perhaps these are all the armies of heaven.

They shout, Hallelujah! This praise of the Lord God Almighty is at the same time as the merchants of the earth mourn the fall of Babylon. The right and proof of God's salvation and glory and power is His judgment of Babylon, the Great Prostitute. His condemnation is just and true because she corrupted the earth by her adulteries.

Hallelujah! God destroys Babylon to avenge His saints.

Hallelujah!

The smoke from her goes up for ever and ever.

The twenty-four elders and the four living creatures that John first saw in Chapter four just after he was caught up to heaven, fall down praising the Lord Jesus Christ for destroying Babylon. Amen, So Be It, the elders and living creatures agree to the judgment of Babylon. Hallelujah, praise God for the destruction of Babylon.

The Lord Jesus Christ is the one seated on the throne, so the voice coming from the throne is probably the Holy Spirit. He commands praise from all who fear him.

vv 6-10) A great multitude in heaven respond with the Hallelujah Handel used in one of the greatest hymns of praise ever written, The Hallelujah Chorus of his Messiah. Their shouts sound like roar of rushing water and like loud peals of thunder.

Hallelujah!

For our Lord God Almighty reigns.

The fall of Babylon ushers in the wedding of the lamb. Let us rejoice and be glad and give him glory! This is the time of the greatest joy and rejoicing since the creation. We are the bride of Christ and we will be clothed in the righteous acts of the saints. The clothing is all that we are told about the wedding supper. This is a time of great blessing. Those in attendance at the wedding supper are blessed. The angel guiding John adds God's authority to what he says. These are the true words of God.

John attempts to worship the angel guiding him. As any faithful servant of God will do, he quickly rebukes John. The angel reminds John that he is a created being as John is. Only God is to be worshiped. For the testimony of Jesus is the spirit of prophecy.

vv 11-18) The woman clothed with the sun, washed in the blood of the lamb, the bride of Christ becomes the armies of heaven as Christ returns to earth to establish His kingdom. Heaven stands open, not only to John but to the inhabitants of the earth gathered together to battle the Lord God Almighty. Deluded by humanistic propaganda, they see the armies of heaven as invading aliens. Rejecting creation, rejecting God's ownership of Earth, they view themselves as the legitimate defenders of the earth.

Ignoring their own sins, they believe that God and the armies of heaven are responsible for the destruction of the earth.

With all of heaven opened to earth, all that John sees is a rider on a white horse. The tribulation opened with a rider on a white horse (6:2) when the first seal opened. Like this rider, the first rider rode out as a conqueror bent on conquest. But the first rider is a counterfeit who deceives the nations and ushers in the reign of the beast. This rider on a white horse is Faithful and True. His horse is an instrument of war in purity.

Like the rider from the first seal judgment, this rider judges and makes war. The antichrist judges and makes war with deception to exalt the proud and arrogant. This rider judges and makes war with justice. Like the vision John saw of Jesus Christ in chapter one, his eyes are still like blazing fire. The eyes of blazing fire penetrate the thoughts and attitudes of the heart. (Hebrews 4:12) His judgments are perfect, both complete and without sin.

At this time the great longsuffering of God is over. Men have been given the entire Church Age to repent. The seventieth week of Daniel is over. For those still unrepentant, God's holiness condemns sin by warring against the hardened sinner. The royal diadems, crowns, that he wears are without number, they are so many. A conquering King adds the crown of the conquered to his own crown. His name is without equal. Though his name is written on him, no one knows it but he himself. He has both the power and the authority to win this war.

His clothing is a robe dipped in blood. John's vision of Christ in chapter one described His clothing as coming down to the feet with a golden sash, the basic garments of a priest. The only acceptable offering for sin is His own blood, which was offered once on Calvary. This blood is the offering of the blood of unrepentant sinners to cleanse the earth. The armies of heaven, however, wear fine linen, white and clean as they also ride into battle on white horses.

His name is the Word of God. Paul tells us in Ephesians 6:17 that the sword of the Spirit is the Word of God. As the vision in chapter one, this rider has a sharp sword coming out of his mouth. In the Church Age, the sword of the Spirit, the Word of God, is used to convict the hearts of men. This sword is used to strike down the nations. The nations, however, will not be completely destroyed at this time because He will rule them with an iron scepter. He now treads the winepress of the fury of the wrath of God Almighty as described earlier (14:19&20) by the angel in charge of the fire of the altar. And the wine press was trodden outside the city, and blood came out from the wine press, up to the horses' bridles, for a distance of two hundred miles.

Though the armies of heaven ride with him, only the KING OF KINGS AND LORD OF LORDS is stained with blood.

On his robe and on his thigh he has this name written:

KING OF KINGS AND LORD OF LORDS.

vv 17-21) This angel standing in the sun cries out with a great voice so that all the inhabitants of the earth can hear and be made accountable. Since the dawn of time, warlords have taunted their enemies before a great battle. This taunt, however, is not figurative. The birds of the air actually gorge themselves on the flesh of all those gathered together to battle the Lord God Almighty. It is the great supper of God.

All the armies of the world amass to fight against the Lord. But the beast and the false prophet are captured. The beast and the false prophet are thrown alive into the lake of fire burning with sulfur. The burning sulfur adds a stench to the pain of the burning flame. No one else, not even Satan, will join them in the lake of fire until the Great White Throne judgment. Finally, the rest of them were killed with the sword that came out of the mouth of the rider on the horse, and all the birds gorged themselves on their flesh.

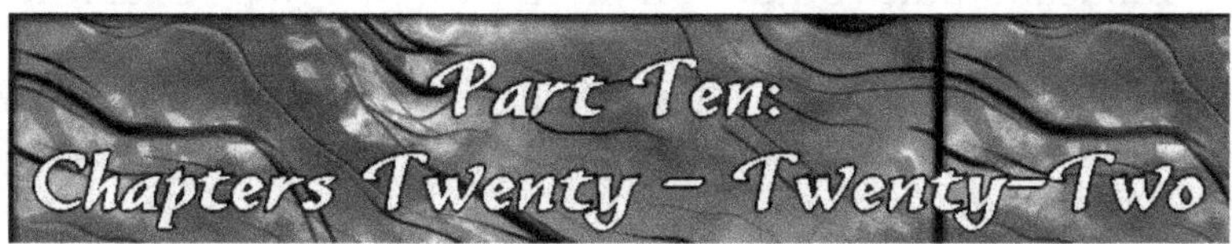

Part Ten: Chapter Twenty-Twenty-two

Chapter Twenty

vv 1-3) After the beast and the false prophet are thrown alive into the lake of fire, an angel comes down out of heaven with the key to the shaft of the abyss. This key to the shaft of the abyss is the same key given to the star that had fallen from the sky to the earth at the sounding of the fifth trumpet. When the fifth trumpet sounded, the star used the key to release the inhabitants of the Abyss onto the earth. This angel uses the key to lock and seal Satan in the Abyss.

The Star of the fifth trumpet judgment is probably Satan himself. Though the passage reads *an angel*, it is difficult to imagine anyone other the Lord Jesus Christ Himself seizing Satan, throwing Satan into the Abyss and binding Satan for a thousand years. This might mean only the spiritual being called Satan, or it might mean his entire spiritual kingdom. The standard interpretation is that all of the forces of spiritual darkness are locked in the Abyss with Satan at this time. Otherwise, demonic forces will be free to roam the earth during the Millennium.

The phrase a thousand years is used 6 times in this passage. It is only used 3 other places in the entire Word of God.

Psalm 90:4:

For a thousand years in your sight
are like a day that has just gone by,
or like a watch in the night.

Ecclesiastes 6:6: Even if he lives a thousand years twice over but fails to enjoy his prosperity. Do not all go to the same place?

2 Peter 3:8: But do not forget this one thing, dear friends: With the Lord a day is like a thousand years, and a thousand years are like a day.

None of these references teach us to use the phrase a thousand years symbolically. Nor is there anything in Revelation chapter 20 that even hints that the phrase a thousand years means something other than what it says.

vv 4-6) Paul teaches us that we will judge angels. (1 Corinthians 6:3) At least some believers will sit on thrones as judges at this time, though this does not say who or what we will judge. Those who had been beheaded because of their testimony for Jesus and because of the word of God during the Great Tribulation are resurrected at this time. The rest of the dead did not come to life until the end of the thousand years. This is the first resurrection. The first resurrection was the saints which arose when Christ arose (Matthew 27:52,53), Christ Himself, the firstfruits, then all the saints from the entire Church age. The resurrection of the two witnesses (11:11,12) and the resurrection of these Tribulation saints are also part of the first resurrection. There is no mention of the first resurrection after this. There is no mention of anyone during the Millennium being part of the first resurrection. This seems to be the end of the first resurrection, strongly implying that anyone who dies during the Millennium will die in unbelief. Christ was the firstfruits of the first resurrection; the rapture is next and finally, the believers martyred during the Great Tribulation. All who are resurrected in this first resurrection will be priests and will reign with Christ and the last enemy to be destroyed is death itself (1 Corinthians 15:24). In the new heavens and new earth there will be no sin in the New Jerusalem, so there will be no death.

The parable of the talents, however, (Matthew 25:14-30) teaches that each saint will have different blessings and responsibilities based on obedience to the Word of God in this life. Some saints will judge, that is, rule over, many cities. Other saints will judge few cities. Some will be just snatched from the fire, that is almost no blessings other than salvation itself. (Jude 23).

The Millennium is for Israel. Ezekiel describes a new temple with restored sacrifices and a river flowing out of the altar to flowing east and west (chapters 40-47). The valley created by the Lord's return when His feet touch the Mount of Olives (Zech 14) will allow this great river to flow to the Dead Sea. The Dead Sea will swarm will fish and flow into the ocean. According to Ezekiel's vision of the valley of dry bones (chapter 37), Israel will be resurrected.

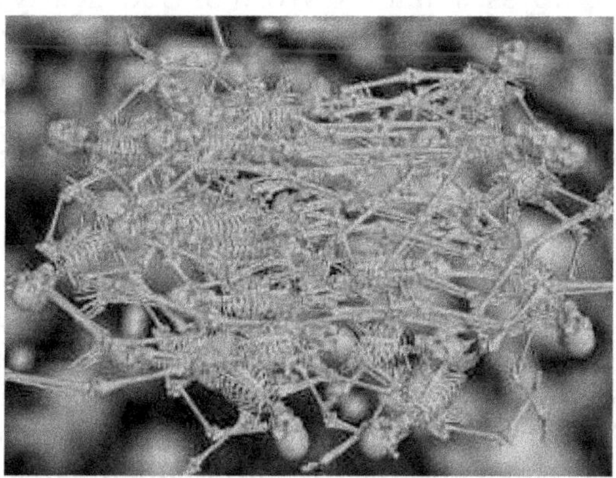

I am going to open your graves and bring you up from them; I will bring you back to the land of Israel. Then you, my people, will know that I am the LORD, when I open your graves and bring you up from them. I will put my Spirit in you and you will live, and I will settle you in your own land. These resurrected Jews will live under their risen King David.

(Hosea 3:5)

Afterwards the Israelites will return and seek the LORD their God and David their king. They will come trembling to the LORD and to his blessings in the last days. "My servant David will be king over them, and they will all have one shepherd. They will follow my laws and be careful to keep my decrees. They will live in the land I gave to my servant Jacob, the land where your fathers lived. They and their children and their children's children will live there forever, and David my servant will be their prince forever.

Instead, they will serve the LORD their God and David their king, whom I will raise up for them.

vv 7-10) John neither covers the Millennium itself nor tells us what calendar is used. We have no way of even guessing the exact number of days. We do not know exactly to the day when Satan will be released from his prison, the Abyss. What the Word of God clearly states is that when his appointed time arrives, Satan will come out and deceive the nations. Though Satan will be unable to deceive the redeemed, he will deceive the nations which are in the four corners of the earth, Gog and Magog. We know nothing about Gog and Magog. The attack of Gog and Magog described by Ezekiel in chapters 38 & 39 is probably at the end of the seventieth week of Daniel. The Gog of Ezekiel is a prince or ruler and Magog is the land to the north. Gog attacks Israel, the land of unwalled villages. The destruction which Ezekiel describes is similar to the judgments of Joel, Zechariah, Daniel and the earlier judgments in Revelation. No one can be certain, however, since we do not know anything about this attack of Gog and Magog at the end of the Millennium. Instead of attacking Israel, John says that at the end of the Millennium Gog and Magog attack the camp of God's people, the city he loves.

No prolonged battle, no opening of heaven, no armies of heaven revealed, nothing but fire came down from heaven and devoured them. Finally, the devil, who deceived them, was thrown into the lake of burning sulfur. At this time the beast, that is the Antichrist, the false prophet and Satan are the only inhabitants of the lake of burning sulfur. This is not a humane prison cell.

They will be tormented day and night for ever and ever. The Lord God Almighty never intended anyone else to inhabit the lake of burning sulfur.

But a holy and just God cannot allow those who refuse His offer of Grace and rebel against His Word to dwell in His presence eternally. The final end of mankind is rebellion against the creator.

vv 11-15) With the Great White Throne judgment, human history as we know it, is over. This judgment is not mentioned anywhere else in the Word of God. We know that the Father judges no one, but has entrusted all judgment to the Son (John 5:22) so this is the Son of God. However, John only says, him who was seated on it. It is white, which shows purity, glory and power. There is only one throne because there is no appeal past this judge. There is no jury, because the Son of God has access to all information so there is no need to deliberate. And the one seated on the Great White Throne has the authority and power to execute the sentence by Himself. The verdict is determined by this life. This throne is only sentencing and execution of the sentence.

Earth and sky fled from his presence, and there was no place for them. There never has been and there never will be any place to escape from the presence of the Lord God Almighty. The word translated sky is the word heaven. This seems to be, with a normal reading, the end of the material universe as we know it. We are not told where the Great White Throne Judgment takes place, only that Earth and sky (heaven) fled from his presence.

Some believe that this means only the end of the earth and the atmosphere, the interpretation the NIV follows. Peter, however, comments on this in 2 Peter 3. The world of that time, the original creation, was deluged and destroyed. The flood only destroyed the world, not the heavens. But the present heavens and earth are reserved for fire. The atmosphere was included in the judgment of the flood, but sun, moon and stars were not. This final judgment of the Great White Throne will include the entire material universe that we know.

Everyone who did not take part in the first resurrection now stands before this throne. John calls them simply the dead. Paul says that our resurrection bodies will be our clothing (2 Corinthians 5:3), because when we are clothed, we will not be found naked. And throughout Revelation the saints are clothed in fine linen, bright and clean. Fine linen stands for the righteous acts of the saints. (19:8). These standing before the Great White Throne have neither. They are completely naked souls, displaying their shame and embarrassment to everyone for all eternity.

Three places are mentioned are mentioned here as the present dwelling place of the unrighteous dead; the sea, death and Hades. Nowhere else in the Word of God is the abode of the damned spelled out this clearly. We can be certain that, without any exception, all will be at this judgment.

The dead will be judged from a set of books, which are their works, and the book of Life. If anyone's name was not found written in the book of life, he was thrown into the lake of fire. Apparently, there will be degrees of punishment in the lake of fire. When their works are judged, the dead were judged according to what they had done as recorded in the books. However, this might only mean that judgment of works, anyone's works, is damnation. As Isaiah said all our righteous acts are like filthy rags (64:6). By the end of the Great White Throne judgment, Hades, the damned and even death itself will be thrown into the Lake of Fire.

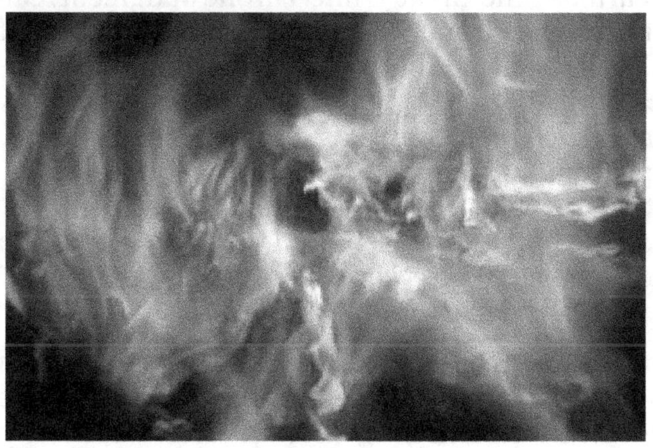

Isaiah in Chapter 66 closes his writings with this description of the Lake of Fire:

"For just as the new heavens and the new earth
Which I make will endure before Me," declares the LORD,
So your offspring and your name will endure.
And it shall be from new moon to new moon
And from sabbath to sabbath,
All mankind will come to bow down before Me," says the LORD.
Then they shall go forth and look
On the corpses of the men
Who have transgressed against Me.
For their worm shall not die,
And their fire shall not be quenched;
And they shall be an abhorrence to all mankind."

The damned will be thrown outside into the darkness, where there will be weeping and gnashing of teeth. Matthew 8:12.

Chapter Twenty-one

vv 1-5) After the Great White Throne Judgment, when all who rebelled against the Lord God Almighty are thrown into the Lake of Fire, God will make a new heaven and a new earth. At the Great White Throne Judgment, earth and heaven flee from God. Again, John repeats here that the first heaven and the first earth had passed away, which fulfill Jesus' often repeated prophecy that heaven and earth will pass away. Pass away probably means complete annihilation, followed by a completely new creation. It could, however, mean a judgment of fire destroying both the heavens and the earth like the flood destroyed the ancient world. The word for pass away simply means depart.

The new heaven and earth have no sea. This sea means both the teaming multitudes of mankind that the Great Prostitute sat on and the great salt waters which we pilot ships across. All life on earth that we know depends on the oceans, so all life will be different from what we know now. The old order of things has passed away. God, the One sitting on the throne commands John to write these words down because these words are trustworthy and true. Once again He says I am making everything new. All that we know about the new heaven and new earth are found in the Word of God. We do not even know if what we call the 'laws' of chemistry and physics will still apply.

The Holy City comes down from heaven to earth where God will dwell with men on earth. Even if this New Jerusalem becomes visible to the inhabitants of the earth when Jesus Christ returns at the end of the Tribulation, it is not the Jerusalem with the rebuilt temple described by Ezekiel. If true, the New Jerusalem will be over the earth during the Millennium because the New Jerusalem after the Great White Throne judgment is coming down out of heaven from God. That would also mean that there would be two Jerusalem's during the Millennium.

Ezekiel prophecies a Millennial Jerusalem with both a temple and sacrifices. Perhaps there will be two Jerusalems in the new heaven and new earth, though that is doubtful since the New Jerusalem will have a great river flowing from it.

The Holy City, the New Jerusalem, is described as a bride beautifully dressed for her husband. This description shows the New Jerusalem as the bride of Christ, which is the dwelling place Christ left his disciples on earth to go prepare.

John 14: In my Father's house are many rooms; if it were not so, I would have told you. I am going there to prepare a place for you. And if I go and prepare a place for you, I will come back and take you to be with me that you also may be where I am. You know the way to the place where I am going.

The New Jerusalem is the home of all the saints of all the ages, not just the Church. Moses, David, Abraham, Noah and Adam will live there, as well as those martyred during the tribulation. This is the dwelling of God on earth. The bride also pictures the close intimate relationship that God will have with all believers for all eternity. The beauty of the city is not the glory and splendor of human cities in this age. Like a human bride, her beauty is both her appearance and her attitude. We, the redeemed saints of all the ages have the attitude, the character which makes the true beauty of the New Jerusalem. As a bride is possessed by her husband so we, the Church, are possessed by God Himself.

The great (loud) voice proclaiming that the dwelling of God is with men is for us. We, all humanity, not just believers, are responsible to know that there will be a new order. God will dwell intimately men.

The old order is sin. Death, mourning, crying and pain are all part of original sin which pass away. Since the God who cannot dwell in the presence of sin dwells with men, sin and the results of sin must pass away. Those who refuse to be washed from both their sin and their sins cannot dwell in the presence of God. As Isaiah said,

"Behold, I will create
new heavens and a new earth.
The former things will not be remembered,
nor will they come to mind.

There will be not even be fond memories of this world of sin.

Only the One seated on the throne has the power and authority to make everything new. He personally tells John to write this down. It is important and we are responsible to tell others this message. God own testimony makes us accountable. We must teach all who will listen.

vv 6-8) The Lord Jesus Christ continues talking to John. Not only is He the only one with the power and the authority to recreate, He is the only one with the power and authority to say so. He swears by Himself because there is none greater. The Lord Jesus Christ tells John what to say and why. There is no separation of powers to keep a certain group of sinners from gaining too much power.

"It is done" is different from "It is finished" spoken from the cross. The provision for salvation was finished on the cross, the sufficient sacrifice offered once for all eternity. However, when Paul wrote to the Romans he said beginning in 8:18:

I consider that our present sufferings are not worth comparing with the glory that will be revealed in us. The creation waits in eager expectation for the sons of God to be revealed. For the creation was subjected to frustration, not by its own choice, but by the will of the one who subjected it, in hope that the creation itself will be liberated from its bondage to decay and brought into the glorious freedom of the children of God. We know that the whole creation has been groaning as in the pains of childbirth right up to the present time. Not only so, but we ourselves, who have the firstfruits of the Spirit, groan inwardly as we wait eagerly for our adoption as sons, the redemption of our bodies.

With "It is done" Christ pronounces the completion of the grand design of human history. With the completion of His work, our healing, our joy will be complete. Human history does not end in judgment. Judgment cleanses the earth to allow God in all His holiness to dwell with men forever.

Once more Christ proclaims His title the Alpha and the Omega, the creator, judge and re-creator of the new heavens and new earth. He offers the water of life to anyone without cost because the cost s so great He alone could pay it. All we must do is admit our thirst and take His offer. By His power we can then obey by overcoming so that we may inherit all this and become sons of God. But no sin can be allowed in the presence of the Holy One. Sinners must have their place in the fiery lake of burning sulfur. This is the second death. With over two hundred words in the Greek New Testament describing various sins, these eight general words include all other sins. The only other place the word fearful or cowardly is used is when Jesus calms the storm and then asks His disciples, “Why are you so afraid? Do you still have no faith?” This is not the fear of the Lord, but unbelief under trials. John even puts the common word unbelief next in this list. This is the unbelieving fear that prevents someone from overcoming. It is selfishness that quenches faith. The vile, or abominable, are those abhorrent in God’s sight. Paul concludes his list in Romans One with them: “Although they know God’s righteous decree that those who do such things deserve death, they not only continue to do these very things but also approve of those who practice them.”

Murderers break the everlasting covenant God made with Noah after the flood in Genesis 9: 5-6:

And for your lifeblood I will surely demand an accounting. I will demand an accounting from every animal. And from each man, too, I will demand an accounting for the life of his fellow man. Whoever sheds the blood of man, by man shall his blood be shed; for in the image of God has God made man.

Isaiah records that murderers breaking the everlasting covenant bring judgment on the entire earth in Isaiah 24:4 and following:

The earth dries up and withers, the world languishes and withers, the exalted of the earth languish. The earth is defiled by its people; they have disobeyed the laws, violated the statutes and broken the everlasting covenant. Therefore a curse consumes the earth; its people must bear their guilt. Therefore earth’s inhabitants are burned up, and very few are left.

The sexually immoral, or fornicators, or immoral persons, or whoremongers are people who have sexual relations of any kind outside of marriage. This is not, as the church of Rome teaches, a general indictment of sex.

God ordained sex but He put it within the boundary of marriage. Hebrews 13:4 says: Marriage should be honored by all, and the marriage bed kept pure, for God will judge the adulterer and all the sexually immoral. Sex is not just to produce children. Sex was designed into the original creation and the imagery of the New Heaven is a bride and her husband. The entire book of Solomon's Song of Songs is devoted to the pleasure of sex within marriage. Chapter Seven, verses 1 and following:

> *How beautiful your sandaled feet, O prince's daughter! Your graceful legs are like jewels, the work of a craftsman's hands. Your navel is a rounded goblet that never lacks blended wine. Your waist is a mound of wheat encircled by lilies. Your breasts are like two fawns, twins of a gazelle. Your neck is like an ivory tower. Your eyes are the pools of Heshbon by the gate of Bath Rabbim. Your nose is like the tower of Lebanon looking toward Damascus. Your head crowns you like Mount Carmel. Your hair is like royal tapestry; the king is held captive by its tresses. How beautiful you are and how pleasing, O love, with your delights! Your stature is like that of the palm, and your breasts like clusters of fruit. I said, "I will climb the palm tree; I will take hold of its fruit." May your breasts be like the clusters of the vine, the fragrance of your breath like apples, and your mouth like the best wine. May the wine go straight to my lover, flowing gently over lips and teeth. I belong to my lover, and his desire is for me.*

The Word of God begins with marriage, ends with marriage, and praises marriage throughout. But those who rebel against the beauty of His design and intent through fornication are placed with unbelievers and murderers in the lake of fire.

Those who practice magic arts, or witches, or sorcerers are next in the list of the eternally damned. Sorcery is the direct worship of evil spirits and the power they can give. It is praised by Disney, folklore, fantasy, science fiction and the entire culture of this world as fun, harmless, even desirable. The Greek word includes those who abuse drugs. These sorcerers are, through the practice of their magic arts, also guilty of idolatry, though many sorcerers deny their idolatry. Idolaters willingly worship something other than the true God. Idolatry through the church age is usually, as Paul told Timothy, people who are lovers of pleasure rather than lovers of God. Or another way Paul described idolaters, this time to the Philippians, people whose end is destruction, whose god is their appetite, and whose glory is their shame, who set their minds on earthly things (NASB).

Jesus Christ concludes this list with all liars. This world believes that "little white lies" are harmless. The Word of God, however, puts liars in the same list as murderers, sorcerers, and adulterers. The ninth commandment, Thou shalt not bear false witness, is not forbidding acting and storytelling. It refers to false doctrines like the Nicolaitans and false witnesses such as those who condemned Stephen. But we can also be liars, bearing false witness, by keeping silent when we should speak out.

These sins are the personal responsibility of individual sinners. Jesus is demonstrating that by rejecting Him, by refusing to allow His blood to atone for their sin, sinners become hardened sinners. As a just and holy God, Jesus points out that those cast into the Lake of Fire are sinners by choice as well as by birth. Rejection of the salvation God provides requires the fiery lake of burning sulfur. This is the second death. It is eternal, without escape, in the torment of weeping and wailing and gnashing of teeth in outer darkness, where their worm does not die and the fire is not quenched. There is no other place for those who refuse to repent of their sins because our holy God cannot dwell in the presence of sin and He will return to earth to once again make the earth His dwelling.

vv. 9-21) One of the last angels to cleanse the earth in judgment takes John away from the throne in the Spirit. This angel, one of the most honored in Heaven, honors John by guiding. He never uses force. The angel simply asks John to come with him to see the bride, the wife of the Lamb. He carries John to a mountain great and high. John's perspective is important, not which mountain he stood on.

Throughout Revelation, Babylon is the Great Prostitute and Jerusalem the Bride of Christ. All of human history is the engagement period. The wedding supper is in Heaven during the Great Tribulation and now John witnesses the final consummation as the eternal dwelling of the saints comes to the earth from heaven after the cleansing of the earth by the great white throne judgment. Everyone is a citizen of one of these two cities. Each of us must decide which city he will be a citizen of. We must either yield to God's Holy Spirit or rebel against His Word by choosing to do what we want.

The Holy City, Jerusalem, is the eternal dwelling of believers. As Ezekiel describes a new earthly Jerusalem which rules the Millennial kingdom, John describes the heavenly Jerusalem which rules heaven and earth forever. Both have a life-giving river flowing out of them, but the river flows from the temple of Ezekiel's Jerusalem. The heavenly Jerusalem has no temple because the Lord God Almighty and the Lamb are its temple. This is the only description of the New Jerusalem in the entire Word of God.

When John first notices the new Jerusalem, she is above him, coming down out of heaven from God. With no point of reference, initially John could not know her enormous size. He begins with the glory of God. The new Jerusalem shines like a star. The word translated brilliance is translated stars in Philippians. Her brilliance was like that of a very precious jewel. Like a jewel, the new Jerusalem has no light of her own, but reflects, amplifies and radiates the glory of God. Jasper is an opaque cryptocrystalline variety of quartz that may be red, yellow or brown. Since the walls and the first foundation stone are jasper, at first the entire city looks like jasper. Unlike the flawed jasper we are familiar with, the New Jerusalem will be as clear as crystal.

The jasper wall has twelve gates, three per side, according to the points of the compass, North, South, East, and West. Each gate is a single huge pearl inscribed with a name of one of the tribes of Israel and each gate has an angel.

Angels are watchers, messengers and guardians. And why even have gates, since they will never be shut? The wall of the city had twelve foundations, and on them were the names of the twelve apostles of the Lamb. Church tradition says that Judas Iscariot's name will be replaced by Paul, not Matthias. While there is a seemingly endless number of applications and 'spiritual interpretations' for this wall, John simply describes the wall and lists the twelve jewels which make up the foundations. These foundation stones will then be decorated with every kind of precious stone.

The angel who measures the gate and the city uses a standard Roman measuring device, the rod. The city is 1500 miles wide, long and high. This could either be a cue or a pyramid. If it is a cube, then the wall will be directly next to it, sort of like an additional layer, 72 yards thick. If the New Jerusalem is a pyramid, then the 72 yards might refer to the height of the wall. If the 72-yard measurement is the thickness, then we do not know how high the wall is.

We do know that the wall around most cities was the tallest structure of the city. The base of the new Jerusalem, 1500 x 1500 miles, is larger than the eastern part of the United States. It will start in the Atlantic Ocean and go far past the Mississippi River, from the

Gulf of Mexico well into Canada. 1500 miles high is 6 times higher than the space shuttles orbit the earth. The city itself is made of pure gold, as pure as glass. The great street of the city was of pure gold, like transparent glass. We must wait for the new heavens and new earth to see real transparent gold.

The central building in Ezekiel's millennial Jerusalem is the temple. John says of the new Jerusalem, I did not see a temple in the city. Throughout human history, worship of the Lord God Almighty has had a barrier. That barrier, sin, is removed by the Lamb and we will be able to worship Him directly. There will be no more need of a temple because there will be no need to atone for sin.

Though John does not say that there is no sun or moon in the new heavens and new earth, the sun and moon are not needed. The glory of God gives it light, and the Lamb is its lamp. With God's glory providing the light, there will be no night there. Peter teaches us that the elements will melt in the heat, so that the existing sun and moon will certainly be destroyed. However, the city will only be one place and only the city itself is illuminated by the glory of God. The rest of the earth might need the sun and the moon.

The kings of the earth will bring their splendor into it. Also, the glory and honor of the nations will be brought into it. And the leaves of the tree are for the healing (service) of the nations. While the word healing is the normal word for mending an injury or curing a disease, it is the root for our word therapeutic. I can mean to assist or help out and it is translated servants or household (KJV) in Luke 12:42. The healing of the nations does not imply that there is still a curse, but that the people of the nations will need something that these leaves can provide. These leaves are not needed to remove the effects of the curse but to provide an additional blessing. These nations will live outside the new Jerusalem on the new earth. Perhaps Isaiah refers to these nations when he mentions the new heavens and new earth. Isaiah, however, says of the heaven and earth he prophecies about he who dies at a hundred will be thought a mere youth; he who fails to reach a hundred will be considered accursed, so he probably means the Millennium. Other than the last chapter of Isaiah, there is no other mention of the new heavens and new earth or these future nations in the Word of God.

Isaiah tells us that we will be able to view the dead bodies of those who rebelled against me; their worm will not die, nor will their fire be quenched, and they will be loathsome to all mankind. Perhaps this is the lake of fire after the great white throne judgment; perhaps hell is visible to those on earth during the Millennium. There is no question, however, that those whose names are not found in the Lamb's book of life will never enter the new Jerusalem. She shall remain eternally pure; nothing impure will ever enter her.

Chapter Twenty-two

vv. 1-5) The last thing John writes about the New Jerusalem is the crystal clear river flowing from the throne of God. Like the river flowing from the temple in Ezekiel's vision, the river is the source of life. This river flows down the great street of the city. The tree of life, kept from mankind since the Garden of Eden, is freely available with twelve different fruits, one for each month. Jesus said that He came to give abundant life. The Holy Spirit is the down payment on that promise. The tree of life is the final installment of that promise. With a few simple promises, John describes what eternity will be like.

No longer will there be any curse. The throne of God and of the Lamb will be in the city, and his servants will serve him. They will see his face, and his name will be on their foreheads. There will be no more night. They will not need the light of a lamp or the light of the sun, for the Lord God will give them light. And they will reign for ever and ever.

Though it is impossible for us to understand everything this means this side of eternity, Jesus concludes this revelation by simply commanding us to trust Him. First the angel told John these words are trustworthy and true. Then the Lord Jesus Himself says, "Do not seal up the words of the prophecy of this book, because the time is near. I, Jesus, have sent my angel to give you this testimony for the churches."

The entire rest of the book consists of blessings for obedience, invitations to believe and warnings for disobedience and unbelief. Revelation concludes with what might be the strongest warning in the entire Word of God. Revelation 22:18 ff

I warn everyone who hears the words of the prophecy of this book: If anyone adds anything to them, God will add to him the plagues described in this book. And if anyone takes words away from this book of prophecy, God will take away from him his share in the tree of life and in the holy city, which are described in this book.

But such a strong warning follows the great invitation "whoever wishes, let him take the free gift of the water of life." And Revelation concludes with Jesus' solemn promise to the church: "Yes I am coming soon."

Come, Lord Jesus!

The grace of the Lord Jesus be with God's people. Amen.

Revelation Study Questions

(Note that the questions are correlated with the original video divisions, which can easily be followed and seen when watching the YouTube segments.) 1. The early Church took a Chiliastic approach to the entire Bible, especially the book of Revelation. What is the modern term for Chiliasm?

2. How is the book of Revelation to be interpreted?

3. What is the best example outside of the Scriptures for the approach John uses in Revelation?

4. What is the double prophecy of Jesus in Matthew 24 which both warns his immediate disciples and announces the Great Tribulation?

5. What is a simple outline of the events of Revelation?

6. What Old Testament book has many prophecies about the same Gentile kingdoms as the book of Revelation?

7. In the prophecies of Daniel what does the word 'beast' mean?

8. The book of Revelation uses symbols which are revealed earlier in the Word of God. What is the 'Sword of the Spirit' a symbol of?

9. What does the Hebrew word, *shabhu `a,* translated 'week' by the KJV in Daniel Chapter Nine, literally mean?

10. What other ways is this Hebrew word, *shabhu `a,* translated throughout the Old Testament?

11. How do we know what the correct translation is for *shabhu `a,* in Daniel Chapter Nine?

12. What happened to the seventieth "week?"

13. According to Daniel Chapter Nine, what event signals the beginning of the seventieth week of Daniel?

14. According to Daniel Chapter Nine, what event happens in the middle of the seventieth week which begins what the book of Revelation calls "Great Tribulation?"

15. According to Revelation, what is the "abomination which causes desolation?"

16. What are the New Testament names for this "ruler which shall come" which Daniel speaks of?

17. What does the number seven stand for throughout the Word of God.

Chapter One Part One

1. What does the word 'Apocalypse' mean?

2. Who was the human author of the book of Revelation?

3. The word 'soon' or 'shortly come to pass' (KJV) actually means what?

4. What does the opening of the book of Revelation contain that is not in the opening of any other book of the Bible?

Chapter One Part Two

1. What will come with Jesus when he returns?

2. Where was John when he wrote the book of Revelation?

3. What is the overall outline of Revelation which John gives us?

4. What does white stand for here?

5. What do the flaming eyes of Jesus Christ in chapter one symbolize?

6. When John writes that Jesus holds the key to death and hades, what does that mean?

Chapter One Part Three

1. What was the geographic location of the churches mentioned in Chapters 2 and 3?

2. What is important about the translation 'lampstand' instead of 'candlestick?'

3. What does the sword coming out of the mouth of the Lord Jesus Christ symbolize?

4. What does the word 'mystery' mean anywhere it is found in the Word of God, including the book of Revelation?

Chapter One Part Four

1. What are the seven stars which Jesus holds in his right hand?

2. How many churches does this letter address by name?

3. Which church is the missionary church?

Chapter Two Part One

1. What is the reason that the seven churches probably do not represent seven successive periods of the church age?

2. Which of these seven churches, according the tradition of church history, was John a member of?

Chapter Two Part Two

1. Which church left her first love?

2. What chapter did Paul write which is called the love chapter?

3. What is the first and great commandment?

4. What is the name of the heresy the Ephesians were praised for opposing?

5. What did the Ephesian church hate which Jesus also hates? *the deeds (practices) of the*

Chapter Two Part Three

1. Which church was the persecuted church?

2. What does the name Smyrna mean?

3. How many days was the church of Smyrna going to suffer persecution?

4. The word 'soon' or 'shortly come to pass' (KJV) actually means what?

5. The phrase 'he who has as ear, let him hear what the Spirit says to the churches' is found at the end of each message to each of the seven churches. What does it mean?

6. The church at Smyrna was materially poor. What were they spiritually?

7. What does God call those in Smyrna who call themselves Jews?

8. What does God promise to give to the believers in Smyrna who are faithful unto death?

9. The church at Smyrna is promised that they will not be hurt by the second death if they do what?

Chapter Two Part Four

1. What city was Antipas put to death in?

2. What city was Satan's throne?

3. What two false teachings did some of the members of this church hold to?

4. If they refused to repent, what would happen to them?

5. Who are the addressees of all seven letters which we call the letters to the churches ?

6. Who dictated these letters to the churches?

7. Who copied down what was dictated?

8. What two sins did Balaam teach Balak to corrupt the children of Israel?

9. Who was Balak?

10. What two things did Jesus promise to the overcomers from Pergamum (Pergamos)?

Chapter Two Part Five

1. Who did the church of Thyatira tolerate?

2. What two sins did her teaching lead servants of Jesus into?

3. What works of the church of Thyatira were praised by Jesus?

4. What is the judgment in Thyatira?

5. What two commands are given to the church in Thyatira?

6. What promises are given to the church in Thyatira?

Chapter Three Part One

1. The church of Sardis had a reputation. What was it?

2. What does Jesus say about them?

3. What does Jesus command them to do?

4. If the people of Sardis fail to obey, what will happen to them?

5. What is promised to those in Sardis who overcome?

6. How can anyone have their name blotted out of the book of life?

Chapter Three Part Two

1. What did Jesus promise to the Philadelphians?

2. What does Jesus say about the Jews in Philadelphia?

3. Since the Philadelphian church only has a little strength, how are we different from them?

4. How will Jesus reward the Philadelphians for their patient endurance?

5. The Philadelphians are told that the New Jerusalem is now with God and will come to earth. Where does it come from?

Chapter Three Part Three

1. What is the Laodicean church known for?

2. Hot means working fervently for the truth. What is someone who is cold?

3. What is Jesus doing for each Laodicean believer?

4. What is the Laodicean believer commanded to do?

5. How do the Laodiceans view themselves?

6. According to Jesus, what was the real state of the Laodicean believers?

7. What did Jesus command the Laodicean believers to do to change the state they were in?

8. How does Jesus prove that he loves the Laodiceans?

9. For every believer who repents, opens the door and let Jesus in, what does Jesus promise to do?

10. What does Jesus promise to give to Laodicean believers who overcome?

Chapter Four Part One

1. Chapter Four begins with John, in the spirit, going through an open door to heaven. What does this represent?

2. From our point of view, when does the rapture take place?

3. The voice talking to John sounded like what?

4. What did the voice command John to do?

5. What did the voice promise to show John when he obeyed the voice?

6. The rest of the book of Revelation is what part of the outline Jesus gives to John in chapter one?

7. What did John see when he got to heaven?

8. How long did it take John to get to heaven?

9. What encircled the throne?

10. What appearance did the one sitting on the throne have?

11. What else was around the throne?

12. What did the elders wear?

13. What came from the throne?

14. What was in front of the throne?

15. What is the correct interpretation of these lampstands?

16. What else was before the throne and under the lampstands?

Chapter Four Part Two

1. Which Old Testament prophet saw a vision of four living creatures, similar to these living creatures?

2. What were the major differences between the living creatures in the Old Testament vision and John's vision?

3. What were the major similarities between the living creatures in the Old Testament vision and John's vision?

4. The Seraphim in Isaiah's vision, which also had six wings, cried the same words as these living creatures which John saw. What did they say?

5. When the living creatures say this, what do the elder before the throne do?

6. What kind of crowns did the elders wear?

7. How many times are the crowns cast down before the throne?

8. What were the Old Testament creatures called?

9. What reason did the living creatures give for worshiping God?

Chapter Five Part One

1. What did He who sat on the throne have in his right hand?

2. Under Roman Law, why would a scroll have multiple seals?

3. Who was able to open the scroll at first?

Chapter Five Part Two

1. What did John do about that?

2. Why?

3. What is necessary to be worthy?

4. Why was the angel continually calling out?

5. Who comforted John?

6. What did he tell John?

7. What limits God?

8. What did John see when he looked ?

9. What does a horn represent?

10. What are the seven eyes?

11. What does the lamb do?

12. Then what does all heaven do?

13. What do the elders have in their hands when they do this?

14. What does the harp mean?

15. What is incense a symbol of here?

Chapter Five Part Three

1. How many angels were praising God and the Lamb along with the living creatures?

2. What is said of the Lamb?

3. What is the Lamb that was slain worthy to receive?

4. Who joins the angels and living creatures in praising God?

Chapter Six Part One

1. What happened in heaven when the lamb opened the first seal?

2. While this brings great rejoicing in heaven, what is the result on earth?

3. While those on the earth view the opening of the seals as judgments, what is heaven's view?

4. What did John see when the first seal was opened?

5. What did this rider have?

6. Who is this rider?

7. The lack of arrows means what?

8. What will he do?

9. Will he be successful?

10. Peace under the Beast will last for how long?

Chapter Six Part One

1. What happened in heaven when the lamb opened the second seal?

2. What did John see when the second seal was opened?

3. What did this rider have?

4. What will he do?

5. What does this mean?

Chapter Six Part Two

1. What happened in heaven when the lamb opened the third seal?

2. What did John see when the third seal was opened?

3. What did this rider have?

4. What will he do?

5. How?

6. What will happen to the poor?

7. What will happen to the rich?

8. What will happen in heaven when the lamb opens the fourth seal?

9. What did John see when the fourth seal was opened?

10. What will this rider have?

11. What will he do?

12. Since there will not be any rapid increase in wild beasts, why are these beasts able to kill men?

Chapter Six Part Three

1. What will happen in heaven when the lamb opened the fifth seal?

2. What will they say?

3. How will they be answered?

4. What will happen in heaven when the lamb opens the sixth seal?

5. What will happen to the earth at the opening of the sixth seal?

6. What will happen to the sun at the opening of the sixth seal?

7. How long will the sun be like this?

8. What will happen to the moon at the opening of the sixth seal?

9. What will happen to the stars at the opening of the sixth seal?

10. How can stars fall to the earth?

11. The sixth seal opening has the moon turn to blood. List the two possible meanings for this.

12. What will happen to the sky?

13. What will happen to the inhabitants of the earth because of these things?

14. What will they say?

15. Why do they not repent?

16. How do unbelievers view these judgments?

17. What is the earthly time frame for the first seal judgment?

18. What is the earthly timeframe for the second, third and fourth seal judgments?

19. What is the earthly time frame for the fifth and sixth seal judgments?

Chapter Seven Part One

1. Why are the 144,000 witnesses introduced after the opening of the sixth seal and before the opening of the seventh seal?

2. What tribe is omitted?

3. Since one tribe is omitted, what tribe is added to make twelve?

4. What does the phrase "the four winds of the earth" stand for?

5. What is the seal used on the 144,000 witnesses?

Chapter Seven Part Three

1. Does the great multitude in heaven include Jews?

2. Does the phrase "after this" mean that each event mentioned is in chronological order from the point of view of people on earth?

3. What is the great multitude standing before the throne wearing?

4. What are they carrying?

5. What washed their robes white?

6. Where did they come from?

7. From Daniel's prophecy, what event starts the Great Tribulation?

8. Where are they when John sees them?

9. What are they doing?

10. Who is with them?

11. What does "Amen" mean?

12. What will the Lamb do for them?

Chapter Eight Part One

1. What happens first when the seventh seal is opened?

2. What does the other angel who stands at the altar have? *a golden censer*

3. What is in it?

4. After that went up before God, what did the angel do with it?

5. What did that cause on earth?

6. What was the purpose?

7. What happens on earth at the sounding of the first trumpet?

Chapter Eight Part Two

1. What happens on earth at the sounding of the second trumpet?

2. What does the word blood mean?

3. What happens on earth at the sounding of the third trumpet?

4. What happens to the inhabitants of the earth because of the third trumpet judgment?

Chapter Eight Part Three

1. What happens on earth at the sounding of the fourth trumpet?

2. What additional judgments are announced by the fourth trumpet?

Chapter Eight Part Four

1. What falls from heaven to earth at the sounding of the fifth trumpet?

2. What does it have?

3. What is it?

4. What is this star?

5. When, in the chronology of the seventieth week of Daniel, is the sounding of the fifth trumpet, the first Woe?

6. What did the star do?

7. What three words describe the unseen spiritual world?

8. What is the first result?

9. Then what happened?

10. What are these creatures not allowed to do?

11. What could they do?

12. What will people under this judgment want to do but be unable to do?

13. Who was the king of these creatures?

Chapter Nine Part One

1. What sound did they make?

2. How could they torment people?

3. What do their heads look like?

4. How else are they described?

5. How long does this first woe, the fifth trumpet, last?

Chapter Nine Part Two

1. What happens in heaven at the sounding of the sixth trumpet, which is the second woe?

2. What happens on earth at the sounding of the sixth trumpet, which is the second woe?

3. What did they look like?

4. What do they do to the people of the earth?

5. How?

6. Since the sixth trumpet judgment, the second woe, is similar to the fifth trumpet judgment, the first woe, how will people on earth know the difference?

Chapter Nine Part Three

1. Up to this point, how many people have been killed since the opening of the first seal?

2. What did the people who remained do?

Chapter Ten

1. What does John see next?

2. How was he clothed?

3. What did he have in his hand?

4. What did he do?

5. Then what happened? *The seven thunders spoke.*

6. What did a voice from heaven command John to do?

9. When John obeyed, what did the voice from heaven then do?

10. What did the voice say would happen to John when he obeyed?

11. What did John do?

12. What was John told as soon as he ate the scroll?

Chapter Eleven Part One

1. Then what was given to John?

2. What was he told to do with it?

3. What was he to exclude?

4. Why?

5. For how long?

6. What is given to the two witnesses?

7. For how long?

8. When does this end?

Chapter Eleven Part Two

1. When does this mean the two witnesses begin their ministries?

2. What did the two witnesses wear?

Chapter Eleven Part Three

1. What else does God call his two witnesses?

2. What are they able to do to their enemies who tries to harm them?

3. What are they able to do to the earth, that is the material universe?

4. What happens to them as soon as they finish their testimony at the end of 1,260 days?

5. What happens to their bodies?

6. Where?

7. What do the inhabitants of the earth do about their bodies?

Chapter Eleven Part Four

1. What happens to their bodies after three and one half days?

2. Who sees this?

3. How do the inhabitants of the earth react?

4. Then what happens to the two witnesses?

5. What was the result of their ministry?

6. Then what happens on earth?

7. What do the survivors do?

8. What is included in the sixth trumpet judgment, which is the second woe?

9. What is the seventh trumpet judgment called in the Old Testament?

10. Is the seventh trumpet judgment the same trumpet which Paul calls the last trumpet in 1 Corinthians 15 or the trumpet of God in 1 Thessalonians 4?

11. When are “the last days?” (Include Scripture references)

12. When the word “day” in the Word of God does not mean a twenty-four hour period of time, what does it mean?

13. What is the first thing which happens after the angel blows the seventh trumpet?

14. What do they say happens to the kingdoms of the world?

15. What do they say happens to the dead?

16. What reason is given for this judgment?

17. What are environmentalists actually doing?

18. What do they say is the seventh trumpet judgment?

19. After they stopped speaking, what happened?

Chapter Eleven Part Five

1. What is next described as appearing in heaven?

2. What is under her feet?

3. What is her crown?

4. What is her clothing?

5. What does word ‘sign’ mean in this context?

6. What does she probably symbolize?

7. What is the male child?

Chapter Eleven Part Five

1. What does the red dragon symbolize?

2. What do crowns and horns symbolize throughout the book of Revelation?

3. What does the color red symbolize throughout the Word of God?

4. What does the number seven symbolize throughout the Word of God?

5. What does the number ten symbolize throughout the Word of God?

6. What does the dragon's tail symbolize?

7. What does a star symbolize?

8. When does the dragon sweep a third of the stars down to earth with himself?

9. Who is the single individual represented by male child born of the woman?

10. What does the dragon want to do to him?

11. What will this male child do?

12. What happened to this male child?

Chapter Twelve Part One

1. What did the woman do?

2. Where did she go?

3. What does this seem to prove about the woman?

4. What is special about it?

5. What will happen to her there?

6. For how long?

7. What is the next event described in the book of Revelation?

8. When does it take place?

9. How do the Scriptures describe the dragon's defeat at this time?

10. Why do the forces of the dragon lose?

11. Where does the dragon go?

12. What are the three other names for the dragon which are listed in this passage?

13. What power is ascribed to dragon in this passage of Scripture?

14. Who is cast out of heaven with the dragon?

15. What happens in heaven because the dragon is cast out?

16. What does it say is now come?

Chapter Twelve Part Two

1. Why?

2. What power overcame the dragon?

3. Who should rejoice because of this?

4. Who has woe because of this?

5. Why is the devil filled with fury?

6. What does the devil do when he realizes that he is cast out of heaven?

7. What was given to the woman to help her escape from the dragon?

8. What is the other time Israel was carried by God on Eagle's wings?

9. Where did she go?

10. How long is a time, times and half a time?

11. Since the word translated here as 'time,' is not used anywhere else in the Word of God to mean a specific period of time, what tells us that it means a specific period of time here?

12. What is important about the place where the woman goes?

13. Since both the woman and the dragon are signs everything connected with them are part of these signs.

What does the river coming out of the mouth of the dragon symbolize?

14. If that is the proper interpretation for river, then what is the proper interpretation for the earth which opens up and swallows the river?

15. Who are the rest of the offspring of the woman?

Chapter Thirteen Part One

1. What is the sea which John sees?

2. What is coming out of the sea?

3. According to the beasts in Daniel's visions, what does a head symbolize?

4. According to the beasts in Daniel's visions, what does a horn symbolize?

5. According to the beasts in Daniel's visions, what does a crown symbolize?

6. What does the number seven symbolize throughout the Word of God?

7. What does the number ten symbolize throughout the Word of God?

8. What is a name of blasphemy?

9. The beast which John saw resembled which beast which Daniel saw?

10. In Daniel's vision, what earthly kingdom did that beast represent?

11. The beast which John saw had feet that resembled which beast in Daniel's vision?

12. In Daniel's vision, what earthly kingdom did that beast represent?

13. The beast which John saw had a mouth that resembled which beast in Daniel's vision?

14. In Daniel's vision, what earthly kingdom did that beast represent?

15. Where did the power for this beast come from?

16. What did he give to this beast?

Chapter Thirteen Part Two

1. In Daniel, as throughout the Word of God, a beast represents human government. What are the two important aspects of a beast at any one time?

2. What does healing the wound as to death mean?

3. Therefore, what are the two possibilities for the "head" of the beast which was wounded as to death?

4. Which seems more likely?

5. What do men do because of the healing of the wound as to death?

6. What do people do to the beast besides worship it?

7. What do people ask each other about the beast?

8. What is the first thing given to the beast?

9. What does the beast do with this gift?

10. How does he use this gift?

11. Who did the beast blaspheme?

12. How long does the beast have to exercise this authority?

13. When does this time begin and end?

Chapter Thirteen Part Three

1. What is the next thing which is given to this beast?

2. What is the last thing which is mentioned that is given to this beast?

3. What will happen to anyone who refuses to worship the beast?

4. What happens when the beast uses these powers?

5. How long has the lamb been slain?

6. What does the phrase 'If anyone have an ear, let him hear' mean?

7. What two things does God affirm with absolute certainty will happen to believers during the Great Tribulation?

8. What does this persecution require believers to do?

9. What are the predominant characteristics of the second beast?

10. Where does this beast come from?

11. What are the two possible interpretations of 'out of the earth?'

12. Whose power did this second beast exercise?

13. This beast completes the unholy trinity. What are the three parts of the unholy trinity?

14. What is the ultimate goal of this second beast? *to cause men to worship the first beast*

Chapter Thirteen Part Four

1. What power does he use to deceive men?

2. What does he order men to do?

3. Later on in Revelation this second beast is given another name. What is this other name for the second beast, the name by which he is usually known?

4. What is the most powerful deceiving sign of the false prophet?

5. What did the false prophet do to the image of the beast?

6. Then what could the image do?

7. What did the false prophet do to anyone who refused to worship the image of the beast?

8. What else did the false prophet do to everyone on earth?

9. What current rampant problem is some sort of permanent identification mark a proposed answer to?

10. What is this mark?

11. What is the number of the beast?

Chapter Fourteen Part One

1. The mark of the beast is a counterfeit. What is it counterfeiting?

2. When John again sees the 144,000, who are they with?

3. Where are they?

4. When he saw them, what did John hear?

5. The 144,000 sang a new song before the throne, the elders and four living creatures. Who else joined them?

6. What is the power of these men?

7. What do they do?

8. What were they offered to God as?

9. After seeing the 144,000 for a second time, what did John see?

10. Where is 'midair,' or 'the midst of heaven?'

11. What is the angel proclaiming?

12. To who?

13. How?

14. From the viewpoint of the inhabitants of the earth, what is the next event on God's timetable?

15. From the viewpoint of the inhabitants of the earth, how long before the skies are torn apart and Jesus Christ returns to earth?

Chapter Fourteen Part Two

1. This simplified gospel only commands that God be worshiped as creator. What does the angel list that people must believe that God created?

2. What happens to anyone who believes this gospel at this time?

3. Who is condemned in the first part of the message of the next (second) angel?

4. Why is she condemned?

5. What is the number of the next angel?

6. As so many other times in the book of Revelation, how does this angel proclaim his message?

7. Why?

8. What image does the angel use to describe how God pours out His damnation?

9. How does this angel describe damnation?

10. According to the message of this angel, who will be damned?

11. At this point in time, what has already happened to anyone who refused the mark of the beast?

12. What does that imply?

13. What are God's saints to do about this?

14. How does John describe God's saints?

15. What does John hear next?

16. Does anyone else hear this?

17. What does the voice say?

18. What does this mean?

19. Throughout the Word of God, who has the title ‘Son of Man?’

20. Where does John see the Son of Man?

21. What is the Son of Man wearing on His head?

22. What does he have in His hand?

23. When is this?

24. Where does the next angel come from?

25. Who does the angel cry out to?

26. Why does the one like the Son of Man wait for the angel instead of acting on His own?

27. What does the angel say?

28. When Jesus was on earth, what did He teach about the end of the age?

29. What are the beast and the false prophet doing?

30. Blood dries rapidly. For blood to be as deep as a horse’s bridle, what must happen?

Chapter Fifteen

1. The seven last plagues complete what?

2. The crystal sea which John saw earlier is now mixed with what?

3. Since the Lord God is not seated on a throne, as John saw earlier, what does that mean?

4. Who is around this sea?

5. What musical instruments do they have?

6. What do they sing?

7. What is the first line of the song of the Lamb?

8. Who sings?

9. What are the tablets of the testimony?

10. Where were they placed?

11. Where do the plagues come from?

12. What are the garments of these angels?

13. What was the temple filled with?

Chapter Sixteen Part One

1. Some people believe the seven vial or bowl judgments are just a heavenly view of what other judgments?

2. Where does God's voice come from which commands these judgments?

3. What is the first bowl judgment on?

4. What is the first trumpet judgment?

5. What is the result of the first bowl judgment?

6. What is the result of the first trumpet judgment?

7. What is the second bowl judgment on?

8. What is the second trumpet judgment?

9. What is the result of the second bowl judgment?

10. What is the result of the second trumpet judgment?

11. What is the third bowl judgment on?

12. What is the third trumpet judgment?

13. What is the result of the third bowl judgment?

14. What is the result of the third trumpet judgment?

15. What is the fourth bowl judgment?

16. What is the fourth trumpet judgment?

17. What is the result of the fourth bowl judgment?

18. What is the result of the fourth trumpet judgment?

19. What is the fifth bowl judgment?

20. What is the fifth trumpet judgment?

21. What is the result of the fifth bowl judgment?

Chapter Sixteen Part Two

1. What is the result of the fifth trumpet judgment?

2. What is the sixth bowl judgment?

3. What is the sixth trumpet judgment?

4. What is the result of the sixth bowl judgment?

5. What is the result of the sixth trumpet judgment?

6. What is the seventh bowl judgment?

7. What is the seventh trumpet judgment?

8. What is the result of the seventh bowl judgment?

9. What is the result of the seventh trumpet judgment?

Chapter Seventeen

1. What is the pure city Jesus is preparing for those who love Him?

2. What is the Satanic counterfeit?

3. Since this Satanic counterfeit is a great prostitute, who is she committing fornication with?

4. What are the many waters on which she sits?

5. The protoevangelium gives us the promise of the savior born of woman. Where is it found?

6. The protoevangelium has what Satanic counterfeit?

7. What is the most famous Greek heroic myth which is one of these Satanic counterfeits?

8. How is that story a corruption of the truth?

9. Who is the first man mentioned in the Bible after the flood to institute this Satanic counterfeit mother/child religion?

10. What is the most famous city which he built?

11. What does Bab-el mean?

Chapter Eighteen Part One

1. What are the two meaning of the word Babylon?

2. Where was John taken to view the great Prostitute Babylon?

3. What color is the beast which the great prostitute is riding on?

4. When does this beast first appear?

5. What Old Testament book has several visions of gentile world kingdoms?

6. List those kingdoms.

7. How many horns are there?

8. What does a horn represent?

9. The message of the angel in Chapter Seventeen is for whom?

Chapter Eighteen Part Two

1. The message of the angel in Chapter Eighteen is for whom?

2. List two Old Testament prophets who prophecy of the Lord's splendor when He returns. *Isaiah, Habakkuk*

3. The mighty shout means what?

4. What do the kings of the earth worship?

5. How do they disguise their greed?

6. When does this take place?

7. God calls to His people to come out of Babylon.

Chapter Eighteen Part Three

1. What is Babylon's judgment?

2. What does God call Babylon's sins?

3. What is God's real heat's desire?

4. Name the last item in the list of Babylon's merchandise.

5. What is Babylon's true nature, as revealed in the Word of God?

6. How long is Babylon's destruction?

7. The punishment of a millstone tied around the neck and cast into the sea is for who, according to the Lord Jesus?

8. What will replace the temporary mirth of Babylon?

9. How many times do the phrases "never again" or "not found again" occur in verses 18:21-23.

Chapter Nineteen Part One

1. As part of the judgment of Babylon, what is the great one word shout in Heaven which is repeated over and over?

2. How long does the smoke ascend from the destruction of Babylon?

3. What do their shouts sound like?

4. What is this preparation for?

5. What is this a time of?

6. What is the one thing John sees about the bride of Christ?

7. Who is the blessing of the wedding supper for?

8. What did John attempt to do to the angel showing him these things?

9. What did the angel do?

Chapter Nineteen Part Two

1. When John saw heaven opened, what did he see? *a white horse whose rider is called Faithful and True*

2. What is His horse an instrument of?

3. What is the Satanic counterfeit?

4. Who follows the Faithful and True rider?

5. Where will be?

6. What are their garments?

Chapter Nineteen Part Three

1. Who is the only one with garments stained with blood?

2. What comes out of His mouth?

3. After he strikes down the nations, what does He do?

4. What is the 'great supper of God?'

Chapter Twenty Part One

1. The angel who comes down from heaven has a key to the Abyss. How does this key compare to the key of the star at the sounding of the fifth trumpet judgment?

2. What is meant by the phrase 'one thousand years'?

3. Who is thrown into the Abyss at this time?

4. Who is seated on the thrones with the authority to judge?

5. Who is part of the first resurrection?

6. Will there be death in the Millennium?

7. What is the end of death?

Chapter Twenty Part Two

1. Who is the Millennium for?

2. What will happen to them?

3. Though the Lord Jesus Christ rules and reigns over all, who will directly reign over Israel?

4. According to Ezekiel, what will be in the middle of Jerusalem during the Millennium?

5. How does the Millennium end?

6. What are these nations called.

Chapter Twenty-One Part One

1. Where does the Devil go at this time?

2. After this earth ends, what happens next?

3. What happens to those whose rebelled against the Lord?

4. What else is thrown into the lake of burning sulfur?

5. According to II Peter 3, what happens at this time?

6. Is anyone exempt from the Great White Throne judgment?

7. What is the basis for this judgment?

8. According to Isaiah in chapter 66, where will this lake of fire be?

Chapter Twenty-One Part Two

1. After the Great White Throne judgment, what does God do?

2. What does John specifically mention as missing from the new earth?

3. Where does the New Jerusalem come from?

4. How large is the New Jerusalem?

5. What is the beauty of the New Jerusalem?

6. What else is made new?

Chapter Twenty-One Part Three

1. What is the difference between the cry from the cross 'It is finished' and the cry 'It is done' when the new heaven and new earth are created? .

2. Why is there no cost for the water of life?

3. According to Jeremiah, what is the everlasting covenant?

4. What does the Word of God begin and end with, which fornication attacks?

Chapter Twenty-One Part Four

1. What word in this list of sins includes drug abusers?

2. What sin finishes the list?

3. What is the second death?

Chapter Twenty-One Part Five

1. Where does John view the descent of the New Jerusalem?

2. Where does the river of flow from?

3. Whose names are on the foundation stones?

4. Whose names are on the gates?

5. What two possible shapes could the New Jerusalem be?

6. What material makes up the New Jerusalem?

Chapter Twenty-One and Twenty-Two

1. Why is there is no need for a temple in the New Jerusalem?

2. The moon and sun are not needed in the city because what takes their place?

3. What is on each side of the river which flows from the throne of God?

4. What are the leaves used for?

5. Since there is no sin in the new heaven and new earth, what needs to be healed?

6. Where do the nations live?

Chapter Twenty-Two

1. Where does the river flow?

2. What will be on our foreheads?

3. Since this prophecy is not sealed, what does this mean?

4. How does the Apocalypse end?

The best gift you can give an author

is an honest, thoughtful review. Please consider leaving one online. Help us understand what you liked and didn't like about the book and why. Help authors reach more readers and spread your influence and ours. If you liked the book, please recommend it to your spouse, friends, pastors, teachers, cashiers, employers, – anybody and everybody you see each day. If you don't know what to say, remember Proverb 16:3 – Commit thy works unto the Lord and thy thoughts shall be established. Thank you!

OTHER BOOKS AND PRODUCTS FROM FINDLEY FAMILY VIDEO PUBLICATIONS

All our books (including Historical Fiction, SciFi, contemporary relationships short stories, and an Archaeological Mystery serial) are linked on our blog.

Elk Jerky for the Soul includes posts on current issues, excerpts from our fiction and nonfiction works, Bible teaching, travel and everyday observations, and more.

http://findleyfamilyvideopublications.com/

Visit our YouTube Channel

https://www.youtube.com/channel/UCGhwNpU115ARMwgYwTIJBrA/featured. Book trailers, video excerpts, project teasers, and more. Science, History, Literature, and biblical worldview studies are the focus of our book and video projects.

Historical Fiction

by Michael J. Findley

The Ephron the Hittite Series (Including boxed set of all titles)

Ephron Son of Zohar

Tawananna Daughter of Zohar

Heth Son of Canaan Son of Ham, Noah

Shelometh Daughter of Yovov Wife of Ephron

Zita Son of Ephron and Shelometh

Adult Romantic Suspense

by Mary C. Findley

The Men of the Realmlands series

Book One: The Baron's Ring

Book Two: The Captain's Blade

Send a White Rose

Chasing the Texas Wind

Carrie's Hired Hand (novella)

Young Adult Historical Adventure

by Mary C. Findley

Hope and the Knight of the Black Lion (plus illustrated version)

The Benny and the Bank Robber Series

Benny and the Bank Robber (Plus homeschool editions for student and teacher with review and vocabulary)

Doctor Dad

The Oregon Sentinel

Lines in Pleasant Places

Science Fiction and Fantasy

by Michael J. Findley

The Empire Saga (all six of the following books in one volume)

City on a Hill and Sojourner (Combined Novella and Short Story)

Nehemiah LLC (Full-length novel available as a standalone ebook, paperback, and hardcover versions)

Empire One: Humiliation

Empire Two: Repentance

Empire Three: Sanctification

Steampunk

by Sophronia Belle Lyon (pen name for Mary C. Findley)

The Alexander Legacy Steampunk Literary Tribute Series

Book One: A Dodge, a Twist, and a Tobacconist (including illustrated version)

Book Two: The Pinocchio Factor

Book Three: The Most Dangerous Game

Book Four: Beware the Bustle

Fantasy/Allegory

by Mary C. Findley

Allegorical clockwork novella inspired by Little Red Riding Hood

The Acolyte's Education

A Paranormal Urban Fantasy serial

His Sign: The Wait Is Over

His Sign 2: The Ezra Solution

Contemporary Fiction

by Mary C. Findley

Romantic Suspense Novella

Fall On Your Knees

Relationships Short Stories

Fifty Shades of Faithful

Fifty Shades of Faithful 2: In Living Color

The Great Thirst Serial Archaeological Mystery (including boxed set of all titles)

Part One: Prepared

Part Two: Purified

Part Three: Pursued

Part Four: Persecuted

Part Five: Persevering

Part Six: Protected

Part Seven: Prevailing

Murder Mystery

Mapped Out Murders

Nonfiction

by Mary C. Findley

Write for the King of Glory, 2nd Edition (updated, with tips on indie writing and publishing)

by Michael J. and Mary C. Findley

The Good, the Bad, and the Ugly: A Readers' and Writers' Guide for Believers

Biblical Studies (Teacher and student editions plus excerpts in OT and NT Manuscript History)

Antidisestablishmentarianism (illustrated and plain versions)

Serial versions, illustrated and plain

What Is an Establishment of Religion?

What Is Secular Humanism?

What Is Science?

What Are the Results of the Establishment of Secular Humanism?

The Conflict of the Ages series (All have teacher and student editions)

I. The Scientific History of Origins

II. The Origin of Evil in the World that Was

III. They Deliberately Forgot: The Flood and the Ice Age

IV. Ice Age Civilizations

V. The Ancient World

by Michael J. Findley

Short Recaps of longer nonfiction works (*Antidisestablishmentarianism* and *Conflict of the Ages)*

Disestablish: An Overview from Creation to the Ice Age

Under the Sun: The Truth about History from the Beginning

*****

Christian Books in Multiple Genres. Join Christian Indie Author ~ Readers Group on Facebook. https://www.facebook.com/groups/291215317668431/

www.ingramcontent.com/pod-product-compliance
Lightning Source LLC
LaVergne TN
LVHW012043160826
845678LV00014B/2687
* 9 7 9 8 2 3 0 3 8 5 2 7 1 *